ROUGH GUIDES

T0085928

POCKET **ROUGH GUIDE**

IRELAND

WALKS & TOURS

YOUR TAILOR-MADE TRIP
STARTS HERE

Tailor-made trips and unique adventures crafted by local experts

Rough Guides has been inspiring travellers with lively and thought-provoking guidebooks for more than 35 years. Now we're linking you up with selected local experts to craft your dream trip. They will put together your perfect itinerary and book it at local rates.

Don't follow the crowd – find your own path.

HOW ROUGHGUIDES.COM/TRIPS WORKS

STEP 1

Pick your dream destination, tell us what you want and submit an enquiry.

STEP 2

Fill in a short form to tell your local expert about your dream trip and preferences.

STEP 3

Our local expert will craft your tailor-made itinerary. You'll be able to tweak and refine it until you're completely satisfied.

STEP 4

Book online with ease, pack your bags and enjoy the trip! Our local expert will be on hand 24/7 while you're on the road.

BENEFITS OF PLANNING AND BOOKING AT ROUGHGUIDES.COM/TRIPS

PLAN YOUR ADVENTURE WITH LOCAL EXPERTS

Rough Guides' English-speaking local experts are hand-picked, based on their experience in the travel industry and their impeccable standards of customer service.

SAVE TIME AND GET ACCESS TO LOCAL KNOWLEDGE

When a local expert plans your trip, you save time and money when you book, even during high season. You won't be charged for using a credit card either.

MAKE TRAVEL A BREEZE: BOOK WITH PEACE OF MIND

Enjoy stress-free travel when you use Rough Guides' secure online booking platform. All bookings come with a money-back guarantee.

WHAT DO OTHER TRAVELLERS THINK ABOUT ROUGH GUIDES TRIPS?

Trip to Spain

This Spain tour company did a fantastic job to make our dream trip perfect. We gave them our travel budget, told them where we would like to go, and they did all of the planning. Our drivers and tour guides were always on time and very knowledgable. The hotel accommodations were better than we would have found on our own. Only one time did we end up in a location that we had not intended to be in. We called the 24 hour phone number, and they immediately fixed the situation.

Don A, USA ★★★★★

Trip to Morocco

Our trip was fantastic! Transportation, accommodations, guides – all were well chosen! The hotels were well situated, well appointed and had helpful, friendly staff. All of the guides we had were very knowledgeable, patient, and flexible with our varied interests in the different sites. We particularly enjoyed the side trip to Tangier! Well done! The itinerary you arranged for us allowed maximum coverage of the country with time in each city for seeing the important places.

Sharon, USA ★★★★★

PLAN AND BOOK YOUR TRIP AT
ROUGHGUIDES.COM/TRIPS

CONTENTS

Introduction

Best itineraries

Directory

Celtic romance

Glimpse the round tower through the Celtic mist at Glendalough (tour 3), enjoy a royal view from the Rock of Cashel (tour 5), climb mystical Knocknarea (tour 15) or discover your inner Skywalker on Skellig Michael (tour 8).

Best Walks & Tours for...

Children

Visit a 19th-century famine ship in New Ross (tour 4), get up close to the animals at Fota Wildlife Park (walk 6) or play games on endless stretches of sand in County Donegal (tour 15).

Gardeners

Powerscourt Gardens (tour 3) are considered among the finest in Europe. Bantry House (tour 7) has terraced gardens overlooking the bay, and do not miss the Palm House in Belfast's Botanic Gardens (walk 16).

Literary types

The Book of Kells can be found at Trinity College (walk 1), alma mater of many great Irish writers, except for W.B. Yeats, who adored Sligo (tour 15). The Dublin Writers Museum (walk 2) will explain why.

Natural wonders

The 40,000 basalt columns of the Giant's Causeway (walk 16), the Cliffs of Moher (tour 11), the view from Croagh Patrick (tour 14) and the waves below Slieve League (tour 15) will take your breath away.

Picture-book villages

Choose from the pretty thatched cottages of Adare (tour 10), Kinvara's stone quays and views of Galway Bay (tour 11), or Lismore (tour 5) with its fairy-tale castle above the wooded Blackwater Valley.

Shoppers

Treat yourself to some Jerpoint Glass in Kilkenny (tour 4) or handwoven linens in Avoca (tour 3), invest in Waterford Crystal (tour 5), or go mad on the high streets in Dublin and Belfast (walks 1, 2 and 16).

Walkers

Walk across heathery hills on the Dingle Peninsula (tour 9), explore the eerie limestone plateau of the Burren (tour 11) or marvel at Connemara's seemingly endless skies (tour 13).

INTRODUCTION

An introduction to Ireland and what makes it special, what not to miss and what to do when you're there.

Discover Ireland

Ireland is Europe's most westerly outpost, swathed with lush, unspoilt countryside dotted with romantic ruins and a dramatic coastline. It also boasts two flourishing and fun capital cities, Dublin and Belfast.

A country deeply rooted in the legacy of its Celtic past; Ireland often appears to be an island of contradictions. While well-known for its world-class cities, it is also wild and remote, and is the westernmost land mass in Europe. This is a country where serried ranges of scantly inhabited hills lead to a formidable Atlantic Ocean on one side and a Blue-flag swimming beach on the other. Throughout your travels, you will regularly encounter the contrast of the old and traditional alongside the new. One pub may be clapping along to the melodic beat of the bodhrán while the next belts out the latest tunes and many a castle or heritage site sits alongside a modernist architecturally designed visitor centre.

Geography and layout

The island of Ireland contains two separate countries: the Republic of Ireland and Northern Ireland. The latter, in the northeastern corner of the island, is part of the UK. In its entirety, the island covers 84,288 sq km (32,544 sq miles), measuring 485km (302 miles) at its longest point and 304km (189 miles) at its widest, while its coastline extends for around 5,630km (3,500 miles).

Low ranges of mountains surround a central lowland area of limestone, much of which is covered in peat bogs.

Getting around

Public transport is a weak point. While the railways link the peripheral towns to Dublin, the lines don't interconnect usefully. Neither is bus travel satisfactory for touring. If you're intending to visit rural Ireland, the only comfortable option is by car.

The routes in this guide begin with two walks exploring the historic and modern faces of Dublin. Following these are a series of drives and walks that have been arranged to run clockwise around the country, down the east coast, along the south and up the west, ending in Northern Ireland. Wicklow, the garden of Ireland, is an easy day trip from Dublin; then the routes visit Kilkenny, Waterford and the iconic Rock of Cashel, all of which are only a short distance from the main Dublin–Cork road. After walking through Cork's medieval streets and Victorian harbour, the routes continue along the scenic coast of west Cork and Kerry to the Dingle Peninsula, before exploring 'castle country' around the Shannon

Beach on Melmore Head, County Donegal

Estuary, visiting Adare, Limerick and Bunratty. The routes then proceed northwards, up the exposed west coast from the strange limestone plateau known as the Burren in County Clare to vibrant Galway city. A day-long drive through ruggedly beautiful Connemara leads towards charming Westport town and scenic County Mayo. Further north, Sligo town and the surrounding countryside were made famous in W.B. Yeats' poems, while County Donegal has beautiful beaches. From here, we cross the border to visit Northern Ireland's fast-changing capital, Belfast, then detour to the Giant's Causeway.

History and architecture

The early settlers left their marks all over the land, from megalithic tombs in the Boyne Valley to the mysterious stone circles of west Cork and Kerry. Later, the flourishing of Irish monasticism in the sixth to ninth centuries bequeathed the beautiful ruins at Glendalough and Cashel. The first hostile invaders were the Vikings in the ninth century, but they, like the Anglo-Normans who followed, intermarried and were absorbed into Irish society. The rich lived in tower houses or castles, like Blarney and Bunratty, fortified against tribal warfare. They also introduced Continental orders like the Cistercians, and endowed monasteries such as Jerpoint Abbey in County Kilkenny.

Henry VIII's decision in 1541 to impose English rule – and what would become the Protestant religion – on Ireland, which shared its Catholic loyalties with England's enemies, France and Spain, had long-running repercussions. Walled towns such as Cork, Galway, Kilkenny and Waterford were used for refuge by English settlers, sent to Ireland to swell the numbers loyal to the king.

The coming of more peaceful times in the eighteenth and nineteenth centuries saw the construction of Georgian Dublin, as well as the elaborate 'big houses' (as the Irish call stately homes) scattered throughout the countryside, many with ambitious gardens.

From famine to feast

Ireland was devastated by the Great Famine of 1845–9, when over a million people died and as many again fled overseas. A century of political unrest, economic depression and emigration followed, during which Ireland haemorrhaged much of its brightest talent. Culturally the Irish have always boxed well above their weight (in art, literature, music and acting) but only relatively recently has the country recovered economically. The development of a robust tourist industry was aided by the availability of inexpensive flights and helped by the handsome scenery getting cameo roles on the big screen, most recently in the latest *Star Wars films*, which featured the rugged West Coast island of Skellig Michael.

A peaceful social revolution in the past decade, when same-sex marriage and

Don't leave Ireland without...

Drinking in a traditional pub. You haven't experienced Ireland until you've nursed a pint of stout while listening to traditional Irish music. Head north of the border, though, for our pick of the pubs: Belfast's Crown Liquor Saloon with its ornate Victorian interior. See page 94.

Kissing the Blarney Stone. Even if it doesn't bestow the 'gift of the gab', it's a dizzying experience. See page 56.

Shopping for Irish crafts. From Waterford crystal to fine linen, and Aran sweaters to traditional jewellery, Ireland is a shopper's paradise. See page 20.

Driving the Ring of Kerry. With stunning coastal and mountain views, this circular drive is simply world-class. See page 62.

Exploring Georgian Dublin. You can still glimpse the Dublin Mountains from the city's 18th-century Georgian squares, as you could when they were built. See page 36.

Walking along a deserted beach. Ireland is blessed with scores of long, sandy beaches. To find one that's empty, too, try counties Sligo and Donegal, in the northwest. See page 88.

abortion became legal both sides of the border, has transformed one of Europe's most conservative countries into one of its more progressive. One thing troubles Ireland's optimistic outlook, however: the potential impact of the United Kingdom leaving the European Union.

Climate

Ireland has a mild maritime climate with temperate summers. July is the warmest month with temperatures averaging 14–15°C (57–9°F), and February is the coldest with averages of 4–5°C (39–41°F).

Rainfall increases as you travel west. Between December and March, cold and rainy weather can persist everywhere. In winter the days are short, with the sun setting at around

4.30pm by the solstice (21 December). In contrast, summer evenings are long, with daylight until 10pm or later. May to August are the best months for hot, sunny weather, but this is never predictable. July and August are the high season for Irish family holidays, and prices and pressure on facilities rise accordingly. The best times to visit are late spring and early autumn; May to June, and September and October.

Population

The population of the Republic of Ireland is 5 million, while Northern Ireland's population is just over 1.9 million. About 1.4 million of the Republic's population live in Dublin, which is fast-paced and stressful (by Irish, if not international standards)

Bar in Limerick

and suffers with gridlocked traffic. Outside Dublin, the average density is 57 people per sq km (148 per square mile). In remote regions like west Cork and Kerry, the average falls to around 27 people per sq km. To get a real feel for Ireland, travel beyond Dublin.

Ireland's population declined during the twentieth century, chiefly due to emigration, and only stabilised in the late-1980s, growing steadily throughout the 1990s. The expansion of the EU in 2004 led to a new wave of immigrants, chiefly from Eastern Europe, but also from Africa and Brazil, where Irish missionaries have long been active in education. While the economic downturn following the financial crisis of 2008 led to a rise in emigration – the Irish economy was fully back on its feet by 2016 (just in time for the Brexit vote in Britain to send shockwaves through the system). The country has staunchly withstood these trials and tribulations though and population figures, and the economy, have stabilised.

Politics and economics

The Republic's two main parties, both broadly conservative, have their origins in Ireland's Civil War (1922–3): Fianna Fáil (*Warriors of Ireland*) traditionally draws its support from small farmers while Fine Gael (*Tribe of the Irish*) is a centrist party supported by many big farmers and professionals. The Labour party is strongest in urban areas, and, beyond their republican nationalist objectives, Sinn Féin also advocates left-wing and progressive social policies. Due to proportional representation, governments tend to be coalitions, but the erstwhile dominance of Fianna Fáil and Fine Gael was destroyed by the 2008 economic crisis. In 2020 Fine Gael formed a coalition with Fianna Fáil and the Green Party, with Sinn Féin making historic ground.

In old Gaelic society people owed allegiance to the tribal chief or *Taoiseach* (pronounced 'tee-shock'). Nepotism was once a part of Ireland's political landscape, but this has changed in recent years. Former *Taoiseach* from 2017–2020, Leo Varadkar, wasn't just a fresh young face when he succeeded Enda Kenny as Fine Gael party leader in 2017, he's also openly gay, and the son of an Indian Hindu.

The Troubles

From 1969, the international view of Irish politics was dominated for thirty years by outbreaks of violence, mainly in localised areas of Northern Ireland, known as 'The Troubles'. This unhappy era began when Catholics in the north started marching to demand civil rights they'd been denied under the Protestant-dominated Stormont government, and were attacked by the Royal Ulster Constabulary (the RUC) and Loyalist gangs. The British Army were deployed to keep the peace, but soon became associated with the Unionists. The Irish Republican Army

Georgian doorway, Dublin   St Mary's Church, Glendalough

Irish literature

The Irish love telling and listening to stories. Before the written word, travelling storytellers (*seanchaí*) entertained beside the fire. The tradition of impromptu verbal wit lives on with Irish comedians and broadcasters. English spoken and written in Ireland differs from English elsewhere, with echoes of Irish-language words and constructions persisting. Jonathan Swift (1667–1745), satirist and author of *Gulliver's Travels*, and dramatist Oscar Wilde (1854–1900) are among the Irish writers whose works continue to be enjoyed worldwide. For a small country, Ireland has an impressive roster of winners of the Nobel Prize for Literature: George Bernard Shaw (1856–1950), W.B. Yeats (1865–1939), Samuel Beckett (1906–89) and Seamus Heaney (1939–2013). Literary festivals are convivial, informal events, where authors and the reading public mingle freely. The biggest one of all is Bloomsday (16 June), a four-day event that commemorates James Joyce's *Ulysses* (1922) in its Dublin setting (see www.bloomsdayfestival.ie).

(IRA) intensified its 'armed struggle' in Northern Ireland, seeking the unification of the island under Irish administration. By 2001 there'd been 3,526 fatalities, about two thirds of them civilians. Eventually, in the late 1990s, peace was achieved through the Good Friday Agreement. British troops finally left the streets of Northern Ireland in 2007, and under joint membership of the European Union (EU), the border became virtually invisible. Protestant and Republican leaders entered a power-sharing assembly at Stormont in Belfast. In 2016 the UK voting to leave the EU rocked the boat again and the power-sharing agreement collapsed in 2017. In 2020 a New Decade New Approach deal was eventually struck.

Economics

The Republic suffered badly from the international economic downturn in 2008, and from revelations of dubious deals among bankers and property moguls. From 2014, the economy rebound and in 2016, the tourist industry saw record visitor numbers. Then in 2020, the Covid-19 pandemic rocked the entire world. It has taken its toll on Ireland with economic growth forecasts swinging from double-digit growth in 2022 to a stable but modest 5%, for 2023 and 2024.

A warm welcome

While nobody goes to Ireland for the weather, it does modern comforts and traditional hospitality well. The Irish have a great capacity for fun and possess a natural courtesy that has disappeared elsewhere. Indeed, most visitors will say the Irish people are what they like best about Ireland.

Enjoying a pint in Dublin

Top tips for exploring Ireland

Newgrange. A large Neolithic tomb in the Boyne Valley near Drogheda, north of Dublin, Newgrange (www.new grange.com) looks like a man-made hill. In fact, it's an amazing feat of pre-historic engineering and one of Europe's best examples of a passage tomb. The narrow entrance tunnel is positioned so the sunrise illuminates the central shrine at dawn on the winter equinox. At its end you can stand in the circular vault and look up at the ceiling to see the remarkable 5,000-year-old technique used in its construction.

National Library. Those with an interest in Irish literature should visit Dublin's National Library of Ireland (2/3 Kildare Street; www.nli.ie). The library's changing exhibitions draw on its vast resources; look out for manuscripts, letters and first editions of Irish writers such as W.B. Yeats and James Joyce.

Joyce Centre. Also in Dublin, fans may wish to make a detour to the James Joyce Centre (35 North Great George's Street; www.jamesjoyce.ie), which showcases editions of Joyce's works, reconstructs his living quarters and displays some of his letters to Nora Barnacle, leaving out the seamier details. The Centre also organises lectures, 'Bloomsday' events (commemorating 16 June 1904, the day in which the events of Ulysses unfold) and walking tours of the city.

Wexford. County Wexford borders Wicklow to the north, Kilkenny to the west and Waterford to the south. Its long coastline boasts many sandy beaches. If you are arriving by car at Rosslare, Wexford town, 18km (11 miles) northwest of the ferry terminal, makes a pleasant stop. It consists of a series of quays parallel to the water and a main street one block inland, with small, old-fashioned shops and pubs. At Ferrycarrig, 5km (3 miles) northwest of Wexford town on the N11, is the Irish National Heritage Park (www.inhp.com). This open-air museum on the banks of the River Slaney provides a useful introduction to Ireland's history and architecture from Stone Age man (6,000BC) to the arrival of the Normans in the twelfth century.

Blasket Island trips. At the tip of the Dingle Peninsula is Dunquin Pier, a steep concrete footpath that spirals down to the sea. A modern ferry (www.blasket islands.ie) makes the 20-minute crossing to Great Blasket Island, weather permitting, a number of times a day between Easter and October. Walk through the island's deserted village and along narrow cliff paths rich in wildlife, and watch the seals on White Strand.

Titanic Belfast. To explore the history of the RMS *Titanic* and its doomed 1912 voyage, go to the Titanic Belfast visitor centre (www.titanicbelfast. com), located in the Harland & Wolf shipyard where the *Titanic* was built.

Café in Kinvara

A Connemara village

Food and Drink

Ireland has an abundance of farm-fresh produce and sea-fresh fish, but only recently has a distinctive style of Irish cooking emerged. A new generation of chefs are creating an exciting new dining experience at all price levels.

Traditionally, Irish food was plain but hearty. Bread and potatoes accompanied the main meal; a meat stew if you were lucky, or fish on Fridays. Vegetables were boiled to a pulp and salads were a rare summer treat. Garlic, avocados and aubergines were unheard of in most homes. However, in one generation, Irish cooking has changed beyond all recognition. There is a new awareness of the amazing raw materials available to chefs in the form of grass-fed beef and lamb, fresh seafood from the Atlantic, abundant dairy produce and home-grown vegetables and salads. Even the humble Irish soda bread, made without yeast or other additives, and once considered inferior to shop-bought white bread, has come to be valued for its delicious wholesomeness. Try it with fresh oysters, a slice of buttered soda bread and a pint of Guinness to understand its appeal or simply enjoy it alongside a hot home-made soup on a blustery day.

Local cuisine

Ireland's high-quality produce is imaginatively prepared by today's chefs to emphasise its freshness, flavour and texture. Ireland's chefs work closely with artisan food producers, who use traditional methods to smoke fish and make charcuterie and farmhouse cheeses. Many restaurants grow their own salads and herbs, or have an arrangement with a local grower. When people eat out, they have come to expect a high standard of cuisine, whether at an expensive restaurant or at the local café.

Irish chefs are trained in the classic tradition, and most go abroad for a few years and bring back culinary influences from their travels – generally Mediterranean, but sometimes eastern – adapting them to the Irish market. This eclectic approach is also followed by Ireland's private cookery schools, the best known being Ballymaloe Cookery School near the famous country house hotel. Darina Allen, its director, has been preaching the doctrine of using fresh local produce, treated with simplicity and respect, since 1983, and has trained many of today's Irish chefs.

Traditional favourites

The fondness for the potato continues to be a national stereotype. The

Oysters fresh from the Atlantic

humble 'spud' will often be served in three different ways – mashed, chipped and dauphinoise, for example. Many Irish people like to order steak when they eat out, and it will be found on even the fanciest of menus.

Many people also eat their main meal – known as dinner – at midday. Pubs advertising 'carvery lunches' offer two or three roast meats carved to order at a self-service counter, with a selection of traditional vegetables, and, of course, spuds. Another favourite is fish and chips, traditionally eaten as a take-away in the street, but now served even in the most upmarket restaurants, like Kinsale's Fishy Fishy. Bread (served with butter on the side) has become a star turn in Irish restaurants, with most places baking their own or buying it in from a specialist bakery.

Farm to fork

All meat in Ireland is now traceable back to the farm, and the flavour of locally reared and butchered meat comes as a pleasant surprise. The Irish Food Board runs a programme, Féile Bia, encouraging restaurants to source as much as possible of their food locally and pass on the information about its provenance to their customers. '*Bia*' is the Irish word for food, and '*féile*' means both festival and celebration. These words on the menu mean that the restaurant is committed to serving carefully sourced fresh local produce. This will often be game in the autumn and winter, such as venison, pheasant, duck and woodcock.

Farmers' markets

Farmers' markets, where producers sell directly to the public, are a great addition to the Irish food scene. They are ideal for picnic food, offering local farmhouse cheeses, charcuterie and pâtés. Traditional breads and baking are also a strong point, as are jams, chutneys and sauces, and fresh organic salads, fruit and vegetables. Check out www.irishfarmersmarkets.ie.

Where to eat

Fine dining

Some fifty years ago, there were hardly any restaurants in Ireland apart from hotel dining rooms, especially in provincial towns. Even today, some of the best restaurants are still to be found in hotels, such as the Park Hotel Kenmare on the Ring of Kerry. Even in Dublin, hotel restaurants are chic, none more so than the Cleaver East at the Clarence Hotel. Many hotels have two or more restaurants, one for fine dining and another informal. They also have the advantage of being open daily, whereas many Irish restaurants close after Sunday lunch and do not serve dinner on Sunday or Monday. Booking is advisable at most restaurants, but even the best, like Dublin's top places – Restaurant Patrick Guilbaud, Chapter One and Sole Seafood and Grill –

Stout and soda bread   Fresh produce at a farmers' market are relatively informal, specifying only 'smart casual' at dinner. If you want to treat yourself, remember that lunch is generally less expensive than dinner. Restaurants often have good value 'early bird' menus for diners who arrive before 7 or 7.30pm.

Bistros, wine bars and brasseries

The Irish have an idiosyncratic way with these terms, all of which can be interpreted as an 'informal, fun place without tablecloths'. A high rate of VAT and high overheads make it very difficult to run a stylish and good-value establishment, but people do try, like Bloom Brasserie on Baggot St, Dublin, the Chart House in Dingle Town or the White Gable Restaurant in Moycullen. An increasingly popular way of keeping prices down is to offer a tapas menu, where dishes can be shared, such as the Market Bar in Dublin. Look out for places that allow you to bring your own bottle (BYOB) and check the corkage charge. Northern Ireland can offer better value, especially if the pound is weak; in Belfast seek out the brasseries along Botanic Avenue for good-quality food at student-friendly prices.

Pubs

Since the introduction of the smoking ban and drink-driving laws, pubs have had to diversify. Nearly everywhere now serves tea and coffee, and espresso machines are commonplace in city pubs. More are serving food, often with an all-day menu that may feature soups, sandwiches, salads and a couple of hot dishes, or at a self-service 'carvery'. The best pub food is found in places that offer daily specials at lunchtime and in the early evening, like the Locke Bar in Limerick city. Most pubs stop serving food at around 9pm, to make more room for drinkers. Some pubs, like Vaughan's Anchor Inn in Liscannor, have effectively turned into restaurants that also serve drinks, with waiter service at all tables. Others, like Moran's Oyster Cottage in Kilcolgan, have a separate restaurant area with a full menu. Children are welcome in most food-serving pubs in the daytime, and some even have play areas and children's menus.

Daytime cafés

Since the Irish acquired a taste for real coffee, cafés have bucked up no end. They usually offer some form of home-baking, often the ubiquitous scone or a warm slice of quiche, as well as sandwiches, salads and home-made soups, and perhaps a pasta option.

Drinks

Irish pubs are expensive. A pint of beer in Dublin will set you back between €7-8 (compared to about €5 in a rural pub), and a soft drink can cost €4–5. Wine by the glass

Oysters in Kinsale

Food and Drink Prices

Price guide for a two-course dinner
for one in the Republic of Ireland:
€€€€ = over 40 euros
€€€ = 30–40 euros
€€ = 20–30 euros
€ = under 20 euros
Price guide for a two-course dinner
for one in Northern Ireland:
££££ = over £40
£££ = £25–40
££ = £15–25
£ = under £15

goes from about €4.50 in a country
pub to €8 or more in a fancy Dublin
hotel. Try to be philosophical: you
are not just paying for the drink,
you are paying for the experience
of being in a real Irish pub. With
any luck, you will get some free live
music (most likely after 10pm), or
some witty conversation for free.

Irish stout
Irish pubs sell the usual range of
beer and lager, bottled and on tap,
in measures of a pint or half pint,
but the one that every visitor has to
try is stout, a strongish black beer
with a creamy white head. Murphy's
is brewed in Cork, but the most
famous stout is Guinness, which has
been brewed in Dublin since 1759.
Great care is taken in storing and
serving it; about three-quarters of a

glass is poured and left to 'settle' for
several minutes, then topped with the
trademark creamy head. In a good
Irish pub it will taste smooth as velvet,
bearing no relation to the Guinness
served in Britain or America.

Irish whiskey
It is spelt differently from Scotch
'whisky' and tastes different too, as
it is triple-distilled from a mixture
of malted and unmalted barley
grains. Irish whiskey has seen a huge
resurgence in recent years, with
popular newcomers such as Kilbeggan
Distillery in County Westmeath
and Dingle Distillery in County
Kerry, although the old favourites of
Bushmills, Jameson and Paddy are
still the market leaders, and all have
a slightly different flavour. The fine
old single malts are generally taken
neat or with a splash of water as a
digestif. Irish whiskey is also used
in Irish coffee, a hot, sweet coffee
spiked with whiskey and topped with
cream, a delicious way to end a meal.

If you have spent too long in the
cold outdoors, there is no better cure
than a hot whiskey, ideally sipped in
front of an open fire. The bartender
should dissolve a teaspoon of sugar in
about an inch of boiling hot water,
adding a slice of lemon studded with
cloves and, of course, a measure of
whiskey. Add more hot water to
taste, and feel the warmth spreading
to the very core of your being.

Irish scones   A delicious fishcake starter

Shopping

Shopping in the two capitals is a pleasant experience, as both have compact centres. Designers use Irish wool and tweeds in high-fashion lines, while traditional craftmakers offer heirloom quality in glass, ceramics, linen and wool.

Both Dublin and Belfast have lively shopping areas, with a mix of department stores, high-street chains and quirky boutiques. In addition, there are shops that sell primarily Irish-made fashion and homewares, which attract Irish buyers as well as visitors. Cork, Limerick and Galway, and smaller towns like Kilkenny, Waterford and Tralee, have shops within the historic centres, so you can combine cultural tourism with retail therapy. Outside the cities, look out for craft shops and galleries with jewellery, leather, ceramics, glass, candles and prints.

Dublin

Shops north of the river are generally less fashionable but better value than those to the south. British chain stores Marks & Spencer, Debenhams and Boots are prevalent. Ireland's version of Marks & Spencer is Dunnes Stores, while Irish-owned Penney's (Primark in the UK) is a goldmine for bargain hunters. Brown Thomas on Grafton Street is an up-market department store for lovers of Chanel, Louis Vuitton et al; it also has branches in Cork, Limerick and Galway.

North of the river

O'Connell Street is Dublin's main thoroughfare, with plenty of shops and attractions. It is home to historic – and long closed – Clerys, founded in 1853 as one of the world's first department stores and under whose iconic clock generations of Dubliners have used as a meeting point. From O'Connell Street, Henry Street runs past the famous Moore Street Market, where colourful characters sell fruit and vegetables with razor-sharp patter. It leads to the Ilac Centre, a large shopping centre, and the Jervis Centre. Arnotts department store, owned by Selfridges of London, is also well worth a browse.

South of the river

No doubt about it, the pedestrianised Grafton Street that runs from Trinity College south to St Stephen's Green is a great deal of fun, renowned for its buskers and street performers. Do not miss the Powerscourt Townhouse Centre to the west, an 18th-century mansion converted into a stylish shopping complex, and the massive glass-roofed Stephen's Green Shopping Centre (with an enormous branch

Irish whiskey

of Dunnes). Grafton Street is a haven for fashionistas, with catwalk-inspired fashion for every budget.

To the west and northwest of Grafton Street, moving towards Temple Bar, you will find streetwear stores and music shops. Nassau Street near Trinity College has a branch of the Kilkenny Shop (Irish crafts and design), and there is a large branch of Avoca Handweavers in Suffolk Street. For Irish ladies' fashion, go to the first floor of Brown Thomas. Nassau Street, Dawson Street and Duke Street are rich in bookshops.

Cork, Limerick, Galway and Sligo

Patrick Street is Cork city's mainstream shopping area, with more interesting boutiques, bookshops and galleries in Paul Street. Limerick's main drag is O'Connell Street; just off it is lively, pedestrianised Cruises Street. Besides its long main street, Galway has two large shopping malls near Eyre Square for more everyday stuff. Revamped Sligo town has an impressive shopping centre, the Quayside, between Lower Quay Street and Wine Street.

Belfast

Belfast has a bewildering choice of shops and, since you pay in sterling, they are often much better value than their southern neighbours. The most recent addition is the Victoria Square Shopping Centre, with its flagship House of Fraser department store, but Royal Avenue and the CastleCourt Centre are also worth a visit. Meanwhile, Botanic Avenue and the Queen's Quarter are filled with quirky bookshops, organic delis and vintage fashion boutiques. The Lisburn Road, to the south, is the destination for designer clothes and chichi home stores.

What to buy

Hand-made crafts are expensive, and you will want to spend some time over your decision, but that is part of the fun. Shop around as you travel, comparing prices and quality. Kilkenny is a good place to start; Kilkenny Design Centre opposite the castle will give you an idea of the high quality and scope of what is on offer, such as hand-made ceramics, hand-loomed mohair or alpaca blankets, fine linen that will last a lifetime and crystal glass, traditionally cut or in modern designs (Jerpoint Glass is superb). Irish-made jewellery also comes in traditional styles (Galway's Claddagh ring, for example). Then there are sweaters and other knitted goods that make good presents. Tweed is made in Connemara and Donegal, and you can still buy hand-knitted sweaters on the Aran Islands, with a label naming the knitter. As well as Kilkenny, you will find a good range of craft shops in Avoca, Blarney, Kinsale, Kenmare, Dingle, Clifden and Westport.

Hand-loomed blankets

Victoria Square Mall, Belfast

Entertainment

Ireland's reputation as an easy-going, party-loving nation is reflected in a packed calendar of arts and music festivals. Dublin is the theatre capital, while traditional music and dance can be found in every corner of the land.

The unexpected success of the Wexford Festival Opera – where international stars attracted large audiences to a small port in southeast Ireland, performing lesser-known operas in the dank Irish October – inspired an ambitious annual calendar of festivals and events. As in Wexford, these provide a buzz for the local community, with plenty of free entertainment, while also attracting visitors and boosting the local economy. While Ireland continues to maintain a high profile internationally in the literary and theatrical world, it also has the dubious kudos of being the originator of one of the world's most successful dance spectaculars, *Riverdance* (1994), responsible for making Irish dancing world famous. For entertainment and nightlife listings, see the Directory.

Theatre

Ever since the Abbey Theatre's production of *The Playboy of the Western World* by John M. Synge in 1907 caused a famous riot (people reacted violently to its use of the word 'shift', referring to a female undergarment), Dublin has had an exciting theatre scene. It also offers great value for money, with tickets at the Abbey starting at €15, often available at short notice. Productions from the Gate Theatre, which fostered the work of Brian Friel, regularly transfer to New York.

Belfast, Wexford, Kilkenny, Waterford, Cork, Galway and Sligo all have well-equipped theatres that host touring productions and sometimes produce their own too. Galway's Druid Theatre Company has successfully transferred productions to Broadway, such as Martin McDonagh's *The Cripple of Inishmaan*.

Language is no barrier at Siamsa Tire, Ireland's National Folk Theatre (Town Park, Tralee, County Kerry; www.siamsatire.com). The titles of the plays are Irish, and the themes are based on Celtic myth and folklore, but the performances are energetic spectaculars, featuring music, song, dance and mime, with no dialogue.

Dance

Before *Riverdance* burst onto the scene, very few traditional Irish dancers made

Irish dancing

a living by toe-tapping. Now touring productions are in great demand, and can also be seen in Irish cabaret at places like Bunratty Castle and the Arlington Hotel on Bachelor's Walk in Dublin. The best way to enjoy Irish dance is to join in a set dancing session; these are like the barn or square dances. Set dancing sessions take place in pubs and community halls, and newcomers are usually welcomed and taught a few steps.

Music

Wherever you travel in Ireland you will encounter live traditional music, most often in a pub. A gathering of traditional musicians on an informal, unpaid basis is known as a *seisiún* (session), and creates its own momentum, as musicians improvise and take flight. Many publicans employ musicians to entertain their customers from about 10pm, and the music is usually free.

Nightlife

Dublin has more than 120 clubs and live-music pubs. The club scene is mainly for the under 35s, who flock to the city from all over Europe in search of a good time. In the rest of the Republic, nightlife is generally an extension of the pub scene; quite literally, as certain pubs in each town are regularly granted a special licence, known as an extension, to stay open until 2am. Ask locally.

Festivals

The festival season opens with Dublin's five-day celebration of St Patrick's Day on 17 March. It was originally introduced because so many visitors were disappointed to find that, unlike the shenanigans abroad, nothing much happened in Ireland on the great day.

Festivals are now a key element in Ireland's entertainment scene. An Irish festival often goes on for a 10-day 'week', including weekends, and aims to entertain all, from children to the elderly. You never know who you will find headlining the list of attractions: a 'local' like Van Morrison, Hozier or Sinéad O'Connor, or a big-name guest from overseas. Cork Midsummer Festival (June), Galway Arts Festival (July), Kilkenny Arts Festival (August) and Belfast International Arts Festival (October) are among the biggest general arts fests. Popular newcomers include the City Spectacular in Dublin and Cork (July), and Galway's Baboró International Arts Festival for Children (October). There are also specialist festivals for classical music and traditional music (known as *fleadh*), and literary festivals galore.

In Belfast you can find traditional city-centre music venues, a burgeoning bar scene in the Cathedral Quarter and shabby-chic music clubs in the student areas of the south.

Temple Bar, Dublin   Fiddler in Belfast

Activities

Ireland has long been a destination for lovers of the outdoors. Initially attracting golfers and anglers, its easily accessible wilderness areas now lure walkers, climbers and cyclists, while its beaches have been discovered by surfers.

Ireland's golf courses continue to be a major magnet for visitors, its traditional links courses joined by swankier developments, such as the Jack Nicklaus-designed course at Mount Juliet. Meanwhile, game, coarse and sea anglers are hooked by Ireland's network of lakes and rivers and long coastline. Walkers are catered for by a range of looped and waymarked walks, cyclists can follow sign-posted trails and surfers can make the most of the Atlantic swell on much of the north, west and south coasts.

Golfing

Ireland has more than 400 courses around the island, including over 30 percent of the world's natural links courses. The Irish are keen golfers, and it is generally seen as an accessible sport of the people, rather than a status symbol. The majority of Irish clubs are unstuffy places that welcome visitors, who are usually pleasantly surprised at the low price of green fees. Exceptions to this are the more expensive parkland courses at the K-Club, Adare Manor and Mount Juliet, and some of the more famous links courses like Lahinch and Waterville.

Angling

The infrastructure of angling centres and boat operators has improved greatly in recent years. Alas, at the same time, water quality has declined all over Ireland. While the old-timers will tell you that the fishing is not what it used to be, Ireland continues to be a popular destination for game, coarse and sea angling.

Walking

There are now 44 long-distance way-marked walking routes, and a network of shorter looped walks, designed so that you return to your starting point within one to three hours. It is easy to escape the crowds in such a sparsely populated country, and you can be walking in impressively wild, uninhabited scenery within an hour or less of landing at the airport. To find a nearby walk see www.irishtrails.ie.

Cycling

Certain towns, such as Westport, Achill, Skibbereen and Clifden have been designated 'cycling hubs', as they provide good accommodation and eating options, along with a choice

Golf is hugely popular

of looped cycling routes suitable for all fitness levels. Organised cycling holidays are increasingly popular, either travelling in a group with a back-up van, or cycling independently to pre-booked accommodation, with baggage transfer. There are also designated mountain-bike parks on forest tracks in rural areas for adrenaline addicts. See www.cyclingireland.ie.

Horse-riding

Ireland rears some of the world's finest horses, from million-dollar racehorses to good-natured, long-haired ponies. Whether you choose a residential riding holiday with tuition on a challenging cross-country course, or a pleasant amble around quiet lanes on a hairy pony, be honest about your abilities, so that the stable can match you with the right horse. See www.ehi.ie.

Adventure sports

Learn sea-kayaking, canoeing, orienteering, rock climbing, abseiling and other outdoor skills at the network of outdoor adventure centres. Send the kids or book a guided family day out. Outdoor enthusiasts will enjoy the annual Killarney Mountain Festival, a carnival of outdoor sport and adventure that takes place each March.

Surfing

Beaches used to be empty in bad weather, except for a few dog walkers. Now they are busy whatever the

Gaelic games

Gaelic games

Hurling and Gaelic football arouse such passions in Ireland that they are often described as a religion. These are fast-paced, high-voltage games, played by dedicated amateurs, organised around the local parish and controlled by the Gaelic Athletic Association (GAA). Hurling is an ancient game played with a wooden hurley, which can propel the ball along the ground, carry the ball aloft on its paddle-like extreme or throw it in the air. It is said to be one of the fastest ball games in the world, and is certainly one of the most exciting to watch. Gaelic football, like hurling, is played by teams of 15-a-side, on the same size pitch, with a round, football-sized ball. It has similarities with rugby and football. Throwing is not allowed. The main season runs from early summer, and culminates in the All-Ireland finals in Dublin's Croke Park in late September. For fixtures, see www.gaa.ie.

weather, with wakeboarders, kitesurfers, windsurfers and, most numerous of all, surfers. A wetsuit is essential. Surf schools offer tuition to beginners on the more benign beach breaks, while the most advanced surfers are towed out by jet-ski, hoping to catch the famous Aileen's wave beneath the Cliffs of Moher, home to some of Europe's biggest waves at over 7.5 metres (25ft).

Surfing off the west coast   Horse-riding in Connemara

Chronology

In just a decade, Ireland has morphed from a conservative Catholic country into a secular, multiracial, progressive society, which has bounced back from the brink of financial collapse. But the Irish know how to ride the wild tide of change – the country's history is full of seismic events.

Early period

c.7,000BC Date of earliest archaeological evidence found along the coast.
500BC Celts migrate to Britain. Ireland's Iron Age begins.
432AD St Patrick arrives as a missionary.
500–800 Early monasticism; Ireland becomes a European learning centre.
9th century The Vikings invade, founding Dublin.
1014 Brian Ború, King of Munster, defeats the Vikings.

English conquest

1169 The Anglo-Normans conquer large areas of the island.
1541 Henry VIII declares himself King of Ireland.
1606 Plantation of Ulster brings English and Scottish Protestant settlers.
1649 Irish Catholic rebellions are viciously crushed by Oliver Cromwell.
1690 William of Orange wins Battle of the Boyne; Protestant rule begins.
1691 The Irish-Protestant parliament introduces the 'Penal Laws' denying Catholics the right to hold public office, own property or vote.

Freedom struggles

1798 Wolfe Tone's Rebellion is crushed by the British; 30,000 die.
1801 Ireland incorporated into the United Kingdom by the Act of Union.
1829 Daniel O'Connell achieves Catholic Emancipation.
1845–9 The Great Famine results in the deaths of around 1 million.
1858 The Irish Republican Brotherhood is founded.
1875 Charles Stewart Parnell elected MP; leads Home Rule movement.
1885 Home Rule is defeated in the House of Lords.
1905–12 The struggle over Home Rule intensifies with the formation of armed militias rejecting it, including the Ulster Volunteer Force.

Independence and after

1916 The Easter Rising is defeated and martial law imposed.
1918 Sinn Féin wins the general election, boycotts the House of Commons and elects the jailed Eamon de Valera as president.
1919–21 Irish War of Independence between the British Army and the IRA.

Carrowmore Megalithic Cemetery, Co. Sligo

Leo Varadkar

1921 Britain and Ireland sign a treaty granting 'Dominion' status to Ireland. The six counties of Ulster remain in UK.
1922–3 The Irish Civil War between pro- and anti-Treaty forces.
1937 The Constitution of Ireland comes into effect, asserting the national sovereignty of the Irish people.
1939–45 During World War II the Irish Free State remains neutral.
1949 Irish Free State leaves the Commonwealth, becoming a Republic.

North and South reconcile

1969 A civil rights dispute in Northern Ireland leads to the armed struggle known as 'The Troubles'.
1972 On 'Bloody Sunday', 14 civilians are shot dead by British paratroopers at a civil rights march.
1973 Ireland joins the European Community (now the European Union).

1990 Mary Robinson is elected the Republic's first woman president.
1998 All parties sign the Northern Ireland peace treaty known as the Good Friday Agreement.
1999 All-party assembly with limited powers set up in Northern Ireland.
2002 The Republic adopts the euro. In the North, direct rule from London is imposed.
2003 Elections in Northern Ireland restore the all-party assembly.

Modern Ireland

2004 The 'Celtic Tiger' boom years.
2005 The IRA declares its war is over.
2015 The Republic of Ireland legalises same-sex marriage.
2016 Britain votes to leave the EU.
2017 Enda Kenny resigns, Leo Varadkar becomes Taoiseach. Power-sharing in Northern Ireland collapses.
2018 The Republic legalises abortion. Michael D. Higgins re-elected President.
2019 Abortion decriminalised and same-sex marriage legalised in NI.
2020 The Covid-19 pandemic hits. NDNA deal struck in NI to resolve power-sharing crisis. New coalition government is formed.
2021 Taoiseach Micheál Martin apologises to victims and survivors of Mother and Baby Homes 1925–98.
2023 President Higgins and Taoiseach Leo Varadkar are the first political figures in Irish history to attend the coronation of a British monarch, at Westminster Abbey in London.

Irish Civil War procession

BEST ITINERARIES

WALK 1
Historic Dublin

This full-day walk covers the main historic sights of Dublin, skirting the banks of the River Liffey and taking in the medieval centre, Trinity College and Temple Bar, one of the oldest – and liveliest – parts of the city.

DISTANCE: 5.25km (3.25 miles)
TIME: A full day
START: Four Courts
END: Clarence Hotel, Temple Bar
POINTS TO NOTE: To reach the starting point, take the Luas (tram) to the Four Courts stop on the Red Line, just behind the Four Courts Building. If you intend to visit most or all of the sights on this walk, consider buying a Dublin Pass. The pass will give you free entry to most major Dublin attractions (see www.dublinpass.ie for details of where you can buy this).

Although Mesolithic and Neolithic peoples occupied settlements in the area in the eighth century BC, it was not until the Vikings arrived in the ninth century AD that Dublin first came into existence. In the winter of 841 the Vikings settled on the banks of the River Liffey. Following the Anglo-Norman invasion of 1169, the Normans built Dublin Castle, and the cathedrals of St Patrick and Christchurch. This tour begins in the very area where the Vikings and later the Normans set down their roots in Dublin.

Modern Dublin straddles the site of two early settlements, Baile Átha Cliath ('Town of the Hurdled Ford', the Irish name first recorded in 1368, which is seen on road signs and buses) and Dubh Linn ('Black Pool', which eventually gave the city its name).

Four Courts

Begin at the **Four Courts** ❶ on Inns Quay, on the northern side of the river. Notable for its large dome and portico, the building was designed between 1796 and 1802 by James Gandon (who also designed the Custom House, further east down the river, and the Bank of Ireland). The name is derived from the four divisions that traditionally constituted the Irish judicial system: Chancery, King's Bench, Exchequer and Common Pleas; this remains the main court building for the Irish Republic.

Cross over the Liffey at the **Father Mathew Bridge**. Looking left towards the city centre, the southern riverbank leads from Merchants Quay to Wood Quay, the site of the first Viking

St Patrick's Cathedral

settlement in what is now the city centre. The settlement was actually sited where the River Poddle flowed into the Liffey, forming a large black pool (*dubh linn*), which was covered up in the late eighteenth century.

South of the river

Crossing onto Bridge Street, you will pass the **Brazen Head**, which claims to be Ireland's oldest pub (established in 1198). From here the road bends left to meet Cornmarket, where you will pass the two **churches of St Audoen**: on the left, the nineteenth-century Catholic church; on the right, a Church of Ireland edifice, built in 1190. The latter, Dublin's only surviving medieval church, is thought to be the oldest of its kind in Ireland. Facing them is the **Tailors' Hall** (1706), Dublin's only remaining guildhall.

St Patrick's Cathedral

Continuing along Cornmarket onto High Street, a right turn takes you down Nicholas Street to **St Patrick's Cathedral ❷** (St Patrick's Close; www. stpatrickscathedral.ie; Mar–Oct Mon–Fri 9.30am–5pm, Sat 9am–6pm, Sun 9–10.30am, 12.30–2.30pm, 4.30–6pm, Nov–Feb Mon–Sat 9.30am–5pm, Sun 9–10.30am, 12.30–2.30pm, with exceptions). A church has stood here since the fifth century, while legend has it that St Patrick baptised converts at a well in the churchyard. The present cathedral was built by the Normans and restored in the mid-nineteenth century; particularly impressive are the enormous flying buttresses that support the magnificent roof. Jonathan Swift, the Dublin-born author of *Gulliver's Travels* and master of prose satire, was Dean here between 1714 and 1745. The well-manicured cathedral gardens are free to visit.

Christchurch Place

Retrace your steps along Nicholas Street to **Dublinia and the Viking World ❸** (St Michael's Hill; www.dublinia.ie; Mar–Sept daily 10am–6.30pm, Oct–Feb until 5.30pm; charge), just past High Street on the left. Reconstructions of medieval street scenes, gory exhibitions of medieval medicine and torture, and interactive presentations of Viking life will keep kids entertained for hours.

Opposite are the gardens of **Christ Church Cathedral ❹** (Christchurch Place; www.christchurchcathedral.ie; Apr–Sept Mon–Sat 9.30am–7pm, Sun 12.30–2.30pm, 4.30–7pm, Mar, Oct Mon–Sat 9.30am–6pm, Sun 12.30–2.30pm, 4.30–6pm, Nov–Feb Mon–Sat 9.30am–5pm, Sun 12.30–2.30pm). Begun in about 1030, Christchurch is the only cathedral of Norse foundation in Ireland or Britain. It was rebuilt in Norman times and remodelled in the 1870s. Highlights include the beautiful, tiled floor and the eleventh-century crypt, the oldest structure in Dublin.

At the end of Christchurch Place, cross over Werburgh Street and

Four Courts dome

when the road forks, take the left one – Lord Edward Street. At the point at which Lord Edward Street meets Dame Street, a right turn just before the **City Hall** (built in 1769) will take you to Cork Hill, and the bright red facade of **The Queen of Tarts**, one of the city's best cafés.

Dublin Castle

Cork Hill Gate is the official entrance to **Dublin Castle** ❺ (Castle Street; www. dublincastle.ie; daily 9.45am–5.15pm; grounds free; entrance to State apartments by 45-min guided tour, charge). Historical evidence suggests that a Danish Viking fortress was built here in around 930AD. The Normans built a wood-and-stone castle in the 1170s; then, between 1204 and 1230, King John erected a larger, stronger castle on the same site. Unfortunately, most of the medieval castle, except for the southeastern tower, was destroyed by fire in 1684. As it stands today, the majority of the castle dates from the Georgian era. Tours of the castle take in the grand State Apartments, the Gothic-Revivalist Chapel Royal and the fascinating medieval Undercroft, the point at which the city walls join the castle below ground.

Follow the signs through the castle grounds to the **Castle Gardens**, site of the 'dubh linn' ('black pool') from which the city derives its name. The Vikings would moor their ships at this spot, where the River Poddle 'pooled'.

Chester Beatty Library

Continuing through the Castle Gardens takes you to the magnificently quirky **Chester Beatty Library** ❻ (Dublin Castle; www.cbl.ie; Mon–Fri 10am–5pm, Sat 11am–5pm, Sun 1–5pm, Oct–Apr closed Mon; free). Permanent exhibitions, taken from the extensive collections of the American mining magnate and art patron Sir Alfred Chester Beatty (1875–1968), include Islamic, Christian, Jewish and Buddhist manuscripts, printed texts, religious artefacts and artworks. There is also a pleasant roof garden, a reading room and a bookshop. The excellent **Silk Road Café**, in the atrium on the ground floor, echoes the museum's eastern leanings.

Trinity College

Leave the castle grounds by Cork Hill Gate and turn right onto Dame Street, which leads straight down to **College Green**, a popular meeting spot.

College Green faces the eighteenth-century Irish Houses of Parliament, which now house the **Bank of Ireland**, completed in 1785 by James Gandon (open during banking hours). A **statue of Henry Grattan** (1746–1820), the Irish parliament's greatest orator, stands in the middle of the green.

Trinity College ❼ (www.tcd.ie) was founded in 1592 by Elizabeth I on the site of a confiscated monastery. Established to educate the Protestant Ascendancy class, Trinity College has

Dublin Castle

educated a host of Anglo-Irish cultural figures. Famous alumni include the historian and statesman Edmund Burke, writer Oliver Goldsmith, and poet Thomas Moore, and more recently Oscar Wilde, playwright J.M. Synge and Bram Stoker, author of *Dracula*.

The Front Gate was built between 1755 and 1759. Passing through it, you will reach the cobbled quadrangle of **Parliament Square**, with its tall (30 metre/100ft) campanile, designed by Sir Charles Lanyon and erected in 1853. On the right-hand side of Parliament Square is a little booth from where you can buy tickets for student-led tours of the College, including the Old Library and the *Book of Kells*.

Trinity College Library

Leaving Parliament Square by the top right corner, you will find (on your left) the entrance to **Trinity College Library** and the *Book of Kells* (May–Sept Mon–Sat 8.30am–5pm, Sun 9.30–5pm, Oct–Apr Mon–Sat 9.30am–5pm, Sun noon–4.30pm, charge). The *Book of Kells*, probably produced early in the ninth century by the monks of Iona, is one of the most beautifully illuminated manuscripts in the world. Its vellum pages contain the four Gospels in Latin, each one decorated with intricate painted illustrations. The manuscript was given to Trinity College in the seventeenth century.

The **Old Library** (1712–32)

Tiled floor of the cathedral

Christ Church door knocker

contains the magnificent **Long Room** (entry included in ticket price). Its high windows let in shafts of glorious light, which rest upon the high bookcases and on the busts of literary and artistic figures that flank them. Changing exhibitions from the library's collections are accompanied by a permanent display of one of the dozen remaining copies of the 1916 'Proclamation of the Irish Republic'.

Leaving the Old Library, turn left to enter the delightful **College Park**. Passing the cricket pavilion on your right, a right turn takes you to the southeastern exit of Trinity College.

Kildare Street and Dawson Street

Turning right out of Trinity along Leinster Street South and taking the first left will bring you to Kildare Street, home of some of the most important buildings in Dublin. The first you will pass is the **National Library of Ireland** (1890) on your left. Next door is **Leinster House** (1746), seat of the two Oíreachtas (Houses of Parliament), the Dáil and the Seanad (Irish Parliament and Senate).

National Museum of Ireland

Like the National Library, the **National Museum of Ireland** ❽ (Kildare Street; www.museum.ie; Tue–Sat 10am–5pm, Sun 2–5pm; free) has a columnar entrance rotunda and was constructed in 1890. Its archaeological exhibitions trace the development of Irish civilisation from the Mesolithic or Middle Stone Age to Late Medieval Ireland; separate exhibitions also showcase artefacts from ancient Egypt and Cyprus. A visit to the museum is highly recommended, if only to marvel at its richly decorated interior.

Literary Dublin

Leaving Kildare Street west via Molesworth Street brings you to Dawson Street, home of the excellent **Hodges Figgis Bookshop** (56–8

Drinkers' Dublin

You can sample two of Ireland's most famous exports at locations near the city centre. The Guinness Brewery, 1km (0.6 mile) to the west, is the biggest brewery in Europe, producing 2.5 million pints of Guinness every day. The Guinness Storehouse (Thomas Street; www.guinness-storehouse.com; daily 9.30am–7pm, July, Aug 9am–8pm; charge) showcases the making and history of the world-famous stout. Admission entitles you to a complimentary pint in the Gravity Bar, the highest in Dublin, with panoramic views over the city.

Alternatively, the Old Jameson Distillery (Bow Street; www.tours.jamesonwhiskey.com; charge) offers various whiskey experiences and is housed in the old warehouse of the 1791 whiskey factory.

Trinity College

Dawson Street; www.waterstones.com/
bookshops/hodges-figgis). This elegant
building contains an excellent selection
of Irish literature and has a well-stocked
'bargain basement'. Meanwhile, **Ulysses
Rare Books** (www.rarebooks.ie), selling
rare books, prints and maps of Irish
interest, can be found on nearby **Duke
Street**, as well as the Duke Pub, starting
point of Dublin's famous literary pub
crawl (www.dublinpubcrawl.com).

Duke Street leads to the pedestrian
shopping area of **Grafton Street**. A
right turn takes you back towards
College Green. Take the first left down
Wicklow Street; you could recharge
your batteries with a tasty vegetarian
treat at **Cornucopia** (19–20 Wicklow
Street; www.cornucopia.ie). Turn right
from here and follow the bend into St
Andrew Street to return to Dame Street.

Temple Bar

Take any right turn off Dame Street
(such as Fownes Street) to reach lively
and chaotic **Temple Bar** ❾. The area is
named after Sir William Temple, who
acquired the land in the early 1600s;
by the early 1700s it had become a
place of ill repute, full of pubs and
prostitutes. Today's Temple Bar still
has the pubs, but the prostitutes have
been replaced by artists, musicians
and film-makers: the entire area was
redeveloped when Dublin was selected
as the 1991 European City of Culture.

Head through busy streets,
avoiding the ubiquitous hen and stag

> ## Food and Drink
>
> ### ❶ Bad Ass Café
> 9–11 Crown Alley, Trinity; www.bad
> assdublin.com; Sun–Thu 10am–
> late, Fri–Sat 8am–late
> This Dublin institution, where
> the late Sinéad O'Connor once
> worked as a waitress, has been
> extensively refurbished but is
> still famous for its burgers. Great
> traditional Irish music. €€

parties, to arrive at the River Liffey.
To the right is the white cast-iron
arc of the 1816 **Ha'penny Bridge**
(officially, the Liffey Bridge), one of
Dublin's best-loved landmarks. The
less exciting **Millennium Bridge**,
to its left, joins Eustace Street in
Temple Bar to the north quays.

On the south bank, west of the
Millennium Bridge, is Wellington
Quay, home of the **Clarence Hotel**
❿. Once owned by Bono and the
Edge from U2, the Clarence is the
landmark building of Temple Bar.
Built in 1852 and refurbished in Art
Deco style, it stands on the site of
Dublin's original Customs House.
The Clarence's **Octagon Bar** is great
for people watching over a pre-dinner
cocktail. For dinner, a restaurant with
a claim to fame of its own – Sinéad
O'Connor was once a waitress there
– is nearby **Bad Ass Café**, see ❶.

Temple Bar graffiti

WALK 2
Modern Dublin

Modern Dublin was shaped by its writers, artists and thinkers. This walk covers the literary, political and artistic sights of the city – from the General Post Office to the National Gallery of Ireland and the Museum of Literature Ireland – to illustrate how Dublin became the culturally vibrant capital it is today.

DISTANCE: 4km (2.5 miles)
TIME: A full day
START: Parnell Square
END: National Gallery of Ireland
POINTS TO NOTE: Many city-centre buses pass close to the beginning of the walk. Alternatively, Parnell Square is a 10-minute walk from Connolly and Tara Street DART stations, and a 5-minute walk north from the Abbey Street tram (Luas) stop. Note that Bewley's Café Theatre is closed on Sundays.

This walk moves from north to south, taking in modern art in the Dublin City Gallery The Hugh Lane on Parnell Square as well as the political and historical monuments of O'Connell Street and O'Connell Bridge before crossing over the River Liffey to the more upmarket south side of the city, with its elegant shopping streets and arcades, green spaces such as St Stephen's Green,

the Museum of Literature Ireland and lovely Georgian architecture.

Parnell Square

Parnell Square, one of Dublin's five Georgian squares, is home to the **Garden of Remembrance ❶** (free). Established in 1966 to commemorate the fiftieth anniversary of the 1916 Easter Rising, it is dedicated to the memory of all those who gave their lives for the cause of Irish freedom.

Dublin City Gallery The Hugh Lane

Right opposite it, the dazzling **Dublin City Gallery The Hugh Lane ❷** (www.hughlane.ie, free) houses modern and contemporary European and Irish artworks. Sir Hugh Lane (1875–1915) established Dublin's Municipal Gallery of Modern Art on Harcourt Street in 1908; the collection was moved here in 1933. There are some 2000 works by artists such as Manet, Monet, Toulouse Lautrec and the twentieth-century Irish painter

O'Connell Street

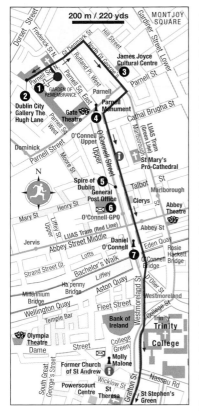

James Joyce Centre

Since 2010 Dublin has been designated a UNESCO City of Literature in recognition of its literary heritage. A fine Georgian house on the north side of Parnell Square is home to the **James Joyce Centre** ❸ (35 N Great George's St; free). The museum is an ode to Joyce and his works and even houses the door featured in *Ulysses* for No.7 Eccles St, the home of the main characters Leopold and Molly Bloom. Right next door is the **Irish Writers Centre** (19 Parnell Square North; http://irishwriterscentre.ie; free) which holds writing courses, talks, writing groups, book launches and readings.

O'Connell Street

Continue on to the end of the street and turn right onto Parnell Street and walk along to the **Parnell Monument** ❹, designed by the American sculptor Augustus Saint-Gaudens and erected in 1903–7. The politician Charles Stewart Parnell (1846–91) became a national hero through his campaigns for Irish Home Rule. However, in 1886, on being implicated in the divorce case of a married woman, Kitty O'Shea, he suffered a dramatic fall from grace. Parnell's legacy was famously debated in James Joyce's *A Portrait of the Artist as a Young Man* (1916) and *Dubliners* (1914).

Continuing south along O'Connell Street, the **Spire of Dublin** ❺ rises up and pierces the sky. With the official title Monument of Light, the

(and brother of W.B. Yeats) Jack B. Yeats. Since 2001 the museum has also been home to Francis Bacon's studio, reconstructed in its chaotic entirety. There is a café here that makes a pleasant stop for morning coffee. Classical music concerts are held on Sunday mornings.

Spire was the winning entry in a 2002 architectural competition to provide a replacement for Nelson's Pillar, which was blown up in 1966 by Irish republicans. It is 120 metres (400ft) in height, and 3 metres (9ft) in diameter at the base, but only 15cm (6in) at the top. Nearby, on the corner with Earl Street North, is a fanciful statue of Joyce.

General Post Office

The Palladian-style **General Post Office ❻**, built in 1818, faces the spire on the western side of O'Connell Street. The GPO was the main site held by rebels during the 1916 Uprising, and it was here the 'Proclamation of the Irish Republic' was read out on Easter Monday 1916. The bullet holes on its columns are a reminder of the bloody legacy of that day. Inside, there is a permanent exhibition space dedicated to the Easter Rising (www.gpowitnesshistory. ie, free). Almost opposite the GPO is the grand building that once housed the historic Clerys department store. Clerys Clock – a long-established meeting point for locals – remains.

Daniel O'Connell monument

Continue south down O'Connell Street and the last statue that you pass is the **Daniel O'Connell monument ❼**. Known as the 'Liberator', O'Connell (1775–1847) successfully campaigned for Catholic emancipation – the right for Catholics to sit at parliament in Westminster – and for the dissolution of the Act of Union between Ireland and Great Britain, which didn't happen in his lifetime.

Crossing the elegant **O'Connell Bridge**, built in the 1790s, will take you over the River Liffey.

Grafton Street and St Stephen's Green

Continuing south along Westmoreland Street, you will pass the imposing **Bank of Ireland** on your right and the grand entrance to **Trinity College** (www.tcd. ie) on your left. Crossing Nassau Street will take you to pedestrianised **Grafton Street**. This area is home to Dublin's most upmarket shops and shopping arcades, like the **Powerscourt Townhouse Centre** (59 South William Street; www.powerscourtcentre.ie).

Bewley's Oriental Café

About 100 metres/yds down Grafton Street, on your right, is recently renovated **Bewley's Oriental Café**, see ❶. Dating from 1827, this Dublin institution is crammed full of teas, buns and Art Deco splendour. **Bewley's Café Theatre** (www.bewleyscafetheatre. com), with performances at 12.50pm every day except Sunday, is highly recommended. Short plays by the likes of Oscar Wilde and Sean O'Casey, or new Irish writers, are performed as you tuck into a light lunch. Be sure to check out the majestic Harry Clarke stained-glass windows, dating from 1928.

Wolfe Tone memorial, St Stephen's Green

St Stephen's Green

After lunch, a short stroll south down bustling Grafton Street takes you to leafy **St Stephen's Green** ❽. At the end of Grafton Street, cross over the road and through the Dublin Fusiliers Arch (1904) to enter the green, which was laid out in 1880. Walking around the green in an anti-clockwise direction, you will see statues of Irish patriot Robert Emmet; writers Yeats and Joyce; the Three Fates (presented to the city in 1956 by West Germany in thanks for Irish aid after World War II); and Wolfe Tone, leader of the 1798 United Irishmen Rebellion. Behind the monument is a memorial to those who died in the Great Famine of 1845–9.

On a sunny day, picnic provisions can be bought from the **Dunnes Stores** food hall in the basement of the Stephen's Green Shopping Centre.

Merrion Row and Merrion Square

Leaving St Stephen's Green by the northeastern gate, turn right to find **Merrion Row**, packed full of trendy cafés and bistros, including **Etto**, see ❷, and **Hugo's**, see ❸.

On the left-hand side is a surprising site: the tiny **Huguenot cemetery** ❾, built in 1693. Tucked in next to the imposing Sherbourne Hotel, the cemetery is usually locked, but you can peer through the railings to see the gravestones of the descendants of the Huguenots, French Protestants who had fled persecution in France. A list of the 239 surnames of those who are buried here can be seen on the wall plaque to the left; this mentions the Becquett family, ancestors of the playwright Samuel Beckett.

Upper Merrion Street

At the end of Merrion Row, turn left

St Stephen's Green

Robert Emmet, St Stephen's Green

Easter Rising

On Easter Monday (24 April) 1916, a motley group of armed nationalists and socialists seized control of buildings throughout Dublin. Standing on the steps of the GPO, the teacher, poet and playwright Padraig Pearse read out the 'Proclamation of the Irish Republic'. A bloody six-day battle ensued between British troops and insurgents, which left a lot of the city centre in ruins before the uprising was finally quashed. The rising lacked popular support, but when the British subsequently arrested 3,430 men and seventy-nine women, and executed fourteen of the leaders at Kilmainham Gaol, the tide of Irish opinion swung in favour of the insurgents. The nationalist movement was re-energised. As W.B. Yeats put it in his poem 'Easter 1916', 'A terrible beauty is born'.

onto Upper Merrion Street, home to **Restaurant Patrick Guilbaud**, see ④, one of the city's most exclusive restaurants. Continuing along Upper Merrion Street, you will see the imposing **Government Buildings** ❿ (www.heritageireland.ie, guided tours only, free; tickets can be collected on the morning of the tour from the National Gallery), housing the office of the Taoiseach (Prime Minister), on your left. Built in 1911 as the Royal

College of Science, the Irish government occupied the northern wing in 1922. The Cabinet Room and the Ceremonial Staircase can be viewed on the tour.

The next building that you will see on your left is the **National Museum of Ireland – Natural History** (www.museum.ie/Natural-History, free), built in 1856.

Merrion Square

Upper Merrion Street takes you straight to **Merrion Square** ⓫, the most famous of Dublin's Georgian squares, laid out between 1762 and 1764. If you're short of time, you can walk straight up Merrion Square West. However, it is worth taking the time to walk anti-clockwise around the streets that line the square. Beginning at Merrion Square South, the houses progress in descending numerical order: look out for the old residences of W.B. Yeats (nos 82 and 52), the playwright Sheridan le Fanu (no. 70) and Daniel O'Connell (no. 52).

The house at **29 Lower Fitzwilliam Street** ⓬ (www.numbertwentynine. ie), on the southeastern corner of the square. The restored house is filled with period furnishings that reflect the lifestyle of a middle-class family in the late eighteenth century, including a traditional cast iron stove in the kitchen.

Oscar Wilde House (closed to the public), on the northwestern corner at no. 1, was the first building to be built here. Wilde, born in 1855, lived here for the first twenty-three years

Georgian doorways, Merrion Square

Food and Drink

1 Bewley's Oriental Café
78–9 Grafton Street; www.bewleys.com
This beautifully restored building is a great spot for coffee, breakfast or a meal, with fresh bread from its craft bakery. The 'James Joyce' balcony and terrace is a favourite spot for afternoon tea (the scones are fabulous). €

2 Etto
18 Merrion Row; www.etto.ie
This tiny restaurant offers antipasti and Italian dishes cooked to perfection at reasonable prices. Particularly popular is 'the worker's lunch'. Award-winning casual dining. €€

3 Hugo's Restaurant and Wine Bar
6 Merrion Row; www.hugos.ie
An award-winning bar and restaurant,
Hugo's offers modern European and fusion cuisine with an emphasis on locally sourced and organic produce. For a less pricey option, try their pre-theatre menu. €€€

4 Restaurant Patrick Guilbaud
21 Upper Merrion Street;
www.restaurantpatrickguilbaud.ie
With two Michelin stars and a reputation for using the finest seasonal ingredients, this is contemporary French cooking at its best. Avoid bankruptcy with the good value set lunch. €€€€

5 The Ginger Man
40 Fenian Street; 01-676 6388
This traditional Irish pub, set over three floors and with an outdoor terrace, has a good range of beers on tap, moderately priced wine, and serves Irish pub-grub. €€

of his life. Just opposite the house on the corner of the park is the whimsical Oscar Wilde Memorial Sculpture by Danny Osbourne, erected in 1997.

National Gallery of Ireland
Cross Merrion Square West into Clare Street. Here, on the left, is the entrance to the **National Gallery of Ireland 13** (Merrion Square West; www.national gallery.ie; free). First opened in 1864, the gallery houses an enormous collection of Western European art ranging from the

Middle Ages to the twentieth century. It houses one of the most important collections of Irish art in the world, including the Yeats Museum (named after Jack B. Yeats, brother of the poet W.B. Yeats) and the Millennium Wing, dedicated to modern art.

For a well-earned drink, retrace your steps along Clare Street and turn left onto Merrion Square West. A right turn onto Fenian Street takes you to watering hole **The Ginger Man**, see **5**, popular with a young studenty crowd.

Oscar Wilde statue   National Gallery of Ireland

TOUR 3
Wicklow

Wicklow, just south of Dublin, is a county of contrasts, where desolate mountaintop roads give way to plunging river valleys. This tour takes in the spectacular scenery of the Great Sugar Loaf Mountain and the Sally Gap, descends into ethereal Glendalough and finishes at the sleepy village of Avoca.

DISTANCE: 75km (47 miles)
TIME: A full day
START: Enniskerry
END: Avoca (or Arklow)
POINTS TO NOTE: Enniskerry is on the R117, 6km (4 miles) south of junction 14 of the M50. If driving from Dublin, the R117 starts south of St Stephen's Green, on Charlemont Street. To return to Dublin at the end of the tour, take the R747 from Avoca to Arklow, and then the N11 north. Alternatively, to get to Kilkenny (tour 4), travel west on the R747 and R727 to Carlow, and join the N9 and N10 southwest to Kilkenny. As this is a scenic mountain tour, with an hour or so between some of the stops, it is worth taking provisions with you. Several points in the tour, such as Glencree and Glendalough, offer excellent walking.

This tour showcases both the spectacular greenery that has earned Wicklow the sobriquet 'the garden of Ireland', and the rugged charms of the granite Wicklow Mountains. It also takes in the Georgian grandeur of the Powerscourt Estate and the mystical delights of Glendalough, one of Ireland's oldest monastic settlements.

Enniskerry and Powerscourt

Begin the tour at **Enniskerry** ❶, a quiet country town built into a hillside, where you can buy provisions for the day and have morning coffee and cake at the delightful **Kingfisher's Kitchen**, see ❶, overlooking the town square (note that there is a free car park off the R117, to the west of the square).

Powerscourt Estate and Waterfall

Enniskerry is dominated by the enormous **Powerscourt Estate** ❷ (www.powerscourt.com), just south of the town. To get there, follow the main road uphill, passing the town square on your right; Powerscourt is clearly signposted off the road. Although the estate dates back to 1300, when the Le

Powerscourt Estate

lifestyle of the super-rich Anglo-Irish during the Romantic period.

There is a separate entrance (and entry charge) for the stunning **Powerscourt Waterfall** ❸, the highest in Ireland at 121 metres (398ft). To reach it, leave the mansion and gardens and turn right uphill; the road twists and turns for several kilometres.

Wicklow mountain drive

Glencree and Sugar Loaf Mountain

Heading back towards the estate, turn left and take the road that skirts the river valley. After about 15 minutes, the road meets the R115. A right turn will take you to the small village of **Glencree** ❹, set into the Glencree valley, with its unusual Peace and Reconciliation Centre (founded in 1974 during 'The Troubles'), former British army barracks and café (see www.glencree.ie).

Glencree affords stunning views, looking east, of the **Great Sugar**

Poer family – later anglicised to Power – built a castle here, the Palladian-style mansion and landscaped gardens that you see today were completed in the late eighteenth century and were restored, following a fire, in the mid-1990s. A visit to the estate gives an insight into the

Powerscourt waterfall   Powerscourt facade

Avondale House

Just outside Rathdrum, on the L2149, are Avondale House and Forest Park (house: Apr–Sept Thu–Sun 11am–5pm, by appointment rest of year; park: daily 8.30am–5pm; free), the birthplace and home of national hero and later disgraced politician Charles Stewart Parnell. The house, built by James Wyatt in 1779 and surrounded by 202ha (500 acres) of tree-lined trails and walks. Don't miss Beyond the Trees – a separate ticketed walkway high in the leafy canopies.

Loaf Mountain, Wicklow's highest point at 503 metres (1,650ft).

Sally Gap
Leaving Glencree, return to the R115 and follow the road south towards the **Sally Gap ❺**. This desolate, barren mountain pass is surprisingly flat, allowing for astonishing views of the steely Wicklow mountains. There is a parking spot 10km (6 miles) further on at **Glenmacnass**, where you can visit a gorgeous waterfall.

Glendalough to Avoca
The road descends to arrive, after another 10–15 minutes, at the river valley of **Glendalough ❻**. At the end of the R115, take a right along the R756 to reach the free Visitor Centre

car park (there is a charge for the higher car park) and the **Visitor Centre** itself.

The name Glendalough derives from Irish Gaelic 'Gleann dá Locha', meaning 'Glen of the two Lakes'; the upper lake, a short walk along the river valley, is much the bigger of the two. St Kevin first established a monastic settlement in 498AD, and monks continued to study and live here until the 1600s. The upper lake has the better scenery and the original sites of St Kevin's settlement and habitations. The lower lake contains many impressive architectural sights, including the monastery gatehouse (the only surviving example of its kind in the country), the tenth-century St Mary's Church and tiny round tower, and a twelfth-century Priest's House.

Leaving Glendalough, a good option for lunch is the **Wicklow Heather Restaurant**, see ❷.

Vale of Clara
Head back along the R756, following the signs to Avoca. After a few kilometres turn right onto the R755 and continue southeast, driving parallel to the Avonmore River. The road descends into the gently wooded **Vale of Clara**, passing through the small village of **Rathdrum**. Nearby are **Avondale House and Forest Park** (see box).

Meeting of the Waters
Some 8km (5 miles) past Rathdrum (taking the R752 south) is the **Meeting of the Waters ❼**, the point

Monastery gatehouse, Glendalough

Food and Drink

① Kingfisher's Kitchen
The Square, Enniskerry; 01-276 4859
Kingfisher's serves freshly made
sandwiches, home-made cakes and hot
drinks to eat in or take away. There's
outdoor seating only (overlooking
the main square), but Avoca blankets
and cushions are provided. €

② Wicklow Heather Restaurant
R756 just before Glendalough (south
side of road); www.wicklowheather.ie
A pub/restaurant on the tourist trail
with prices to match. The menu is much
better value at lunch, when you can get
a goat's cheese open sandwich or a
crispy chicken salad, as well as mains
and specials. You can enjoy your meal
on the pleasant outdoor terrace. €€

③ Avoca Handweavers Café and Store
The Mill at Avoca Village; www.avoca.com
Inside the Avoca Handweavers
is a retro-style café and deli,
selling delicious tea, cakes,
soup and sandwiches. €

④ Hendley's Fish and Chip Restaurant and Takeaway
Avoca Village; 0402-30937
More than your average fish-and-
chip restaurant, Hendley's serves
the 'daily catch' as well as smoked
fish specials at very reasonable
prices. Right on the river. €

at which the rivers Avonbeg and
Avonmore converge to form the River
Avoca. Set deep in the Vale of Avoca,
this is a surprisingly moody place,
blanketed by trees. Thomas Moore
gave the spot its name in an 1808
poem, which is inscribed on a wall.

Avoca
A few minutes further on, set just off
the main road alongside the river, is
delightful **Avoca ❽**. Once the location
for the 1990s BBC series *Ballykissangel*,
the main draw of the village is now
Avoca Handweavers (Old Mill, Main
Street; www.avoca.com). The weavers
here have been producing linens from
Ireland's oldest working mill since
1723; you can see them in action in
the weaving sheds. The fruits of their
labours – including rugs and bed linen,
clothing and accessories – are sold
here in the mill shop, and in stores
throughout Ireland. The mill also has
an excellent **café**, see ③. For fish and
chips, **Hendley's**, opposite Fitzgerald's
pub, is a good option – see ④.

Arklow
Continue southeast from Avoca along
the R747 to **Arklow ❾**, Wicklow's
busiest town and once a thriving port.

Avoca Handweavers

Glendalough lower lake scenery

TOUR 4
Kilkenny

Explore Kilkenny's castle and attractive medieval centre before driving through picturesque villages on the River Nore to tranquil Jerpoint Abbey just outside of Thomastown. Finish off aboard a famine ship at New Ross in County Wexford.

DISTANCE: City walk: 2km (1.2 miles); drive: 46km (28.5 miles)
TIME: A 2-hour city walk followed by a half-day drive
START: Kilkenny city
END: New Ross
POINTS TO NOTE: Kilkenny is 116km (72 miles) southwest of Dublin and approximately 100km (62 miles) west of Arklow. New Ross is 14km (8 miles) northeast of Waterford, starting point of tour 5, and 53km (33 miles) west of Rosslare ferry terminal.

Kilkenny city

Kilkenny ❶ was founded by St Canice in the sixth century and at times rivalled Dublin. However, the Hiberno-Norman lords, worried their influence was waning, passed the Statutes of Kilkenny in 1366, to prevent English settlers speaking Irish and intermarrying with locals. The compact centre has several medieval buildings and cobbled alleyways off the main street known as 'slips', but the star of the show is Kilkenny Castle, set in parklands beside the River Nore.

Kilkenny Castle

Follow signs for the city centre which will lead you to **Kilkenny Castle ❶** (www.kilkennycastle.ie, charge, gardens free), an unmistakable landmark beside a large public car park. The original castle was built in the thirteenth century, but the present building dates mainly from 1820. Inside its huge entrance gate you are greeted by a magnificent panorama in which the mature trees of the castle's parklands frame the distant countryside, with a formal rose garden and fountain in the foreground. The seat of the Butler family (the Dukes of Ormond), two wings of the castle have been restored in the style of a grand country house circa 1830. They contain a library, drawing room and long gallery.

Kilkenny Design Craft Centre

Cross the road in front of the castle to visit its stable block, an elegant semi-circular construction in the

Kilkenny Castle

Medieval town centre

Turn left out of the Design Centre, past some fine eighteenth-century houses along the Parade, and turn right at the traffic lights onto Rose Inn Street. Take the first left onto St Mary's Lane and you'll arrive at **Shee Alms House** **C**, a stone building constructed in 1594 to house the poor, and now the **Tourist Information Office**. From here, head onto St Mary's Lane to the **Medieval Mile Museum D** where you can enjoy a guided tour. Exiting the museum, head straight out onto the bustling High Street and turn right to walk past the **Tholsel** **E**, Kilkenny's former toll house, which was built in 1761 and has an arcade over the pavement and an octagonal clock tower. Further down on the opposite side of the road, is **Rothe House and Garden** **F** (Parliament Street; www.rothehouse. com) a sixteenth-century merchant's fortified home, which houses an interesting museum of local history. It's one of the city's real treasures.

classical style, topped by a copper dome and weathervane. It now houses the **Kilkenny Design Craft Centre** **B** (www.kilkennydesign. com), one of Ireland's best craft shops and a nice resturant. Also here is the headquarters of the Crafts Council of Ireland, which holds regular exhibitions of contemporary craftwork (free). There are also several small craft studios and factory outlets. A gate at the rear leads to the pleasant gardens of **Butler House** (www.butler. ie), the castle's dower house.

Kilkenny Design Craft Centre

St Canice's Cathedral

From Rothe House, on your left you can see **St Canice's Cathedral** **F** (www.stcanicescathedral.ie), named after the city's founder, on a height above the town. It is approached from Parliament Street up a flight of stone steps and under an arch. The cathedral, with its massive round tower and stepped battlements, dates from the thirteenth century, and is believed to be on the site of St Canice's monastic foundation. Oliver Cromwell's soldiers left it a roofless ruin, and it has been much restored over the years, but it still has some fine medieval monuments. Wooden steps inside the 30-metre (98ft) tall **round tower** can be climbed (no children under 12).

Black Abbey

Leave the cathedral by the main gate leading to Dean Street. Cross over and follow the finger signpost down an alley that crosses a canal to the **Dominican Church**. It incorporates the slender tower and fourteenth-century windows of the **Black Abbey** **G**, dating from 1225; in the forecourt is an unusual collection of mid-thirteenth-century stone coffins.

Turn left out of the church and follow the 'slip' back to Parliament Street. Turn right, and at the fork take the lower street, St Kieran's, a lively pedestrianised area filled with cafés as well as the famed **Kyteler's Inn**. You can follow it straight back to Rose Inn Street and the castle or cut up the Butterslip back onto the High Street.

Nore Valley

Head straight out of town from the castle and join the R700, a pretty minor road that follows the River Nore southwards to its estuary.

Bennettsbridge

The stone bridge at **Bennettsbridge** **2**, 6km (4 miles) south of Kilkenny, dates from 1285 and is one of the oldest crossings of the River Nore. The road swings right over the bridge, and passes **Nicholas Mosse Pottery** (www.nicholasmosse.com), which sells handmade pottery and is a major stop on the Trail Kilkenny's **Food and Craft Experience Trail** (www.trailkilkenny.ie).

Thomastown and Jerpoint Abbey

Thomastown **3**, 12km (7 miles) further south, is an attractive village of greystone buildings and steep hills that dates from the thirteenth century. You could stop for lunch here at the **Blackberry Café**, see **1**.

Follow the signs in the town for a 2km (1-mile) detour southwest across the bridge to **Jerpoint Abbey** **4** (www. heritageireland.ie). Founded in 1158 by the Cistercians, this is one of the finest monastic ruins in Ireland, consisting of a cloister, quadrangle and three-naved church with Romanesque arches. Walk around the two sides of the cloisters to appreciate their unusual carvings.

The Tholsel

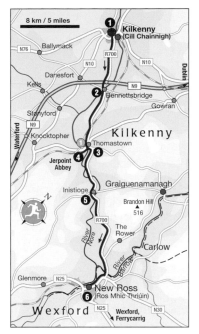

Food and Drink

1 The Blackberry Café
Market Street, Thomastown;
056-772 4690
This small café sits on the corner in
the centre of the town. Enjoy breakfast
or a delicious lunch of soup, great
sandwiches, salads and homemade
cakes to have in or take away. €

with a view of the picturesque bridge
backed by a line of Georgian houses
or follow the signs up the hill to
Woodstock House & Gardens.

New Ross

Continue along the R700 for another
17km (10.5 miles), crossing the border
into County Wexford at **New Ross**
6. The town was built on a steep
hill overlooking the River Barrow.
On the riverbank you will see the tall
masts of the ***Dunbrody Famine Ship***
(www.dunbrody.com; charge for tours),
a full-scale replica of a sailing ship
built in 1845 to transport emigrants
to North America. On board, actors
recount stories of the hundreds of
passengers desperate to escape the
Great Famine. The real *Dunbrody*
had a good captain and record, but
on many vessels, known as 'coffin-
ships', conditions were appalling. The
experience is both entertaining and a
sobering reminder of harsh times.

Inistioge

Return to Thomastown and re-join the
R700 south, crossing the Nore again via
a long, 12-arched stone bridge, amid
sweeping views of a wooded valley, the
location of **Inistioge** 5. The village
is situated on a bend of the river and
has a tree-lined square leading to a tall
stone bridge. It's a favourite location
for films. You can either follow the road
to the left at the **Woodstock Arms** for
the riverfront. A flat grassy area next to
the river is a perfect spot for picnicking,

Jerpoint Abbey   St Canice's Cathedral

TOUR 5
Waterford and the Rock of Cashel

Explore Waterford city's eighteenth-century quayside then drive to the iconic Rock of Cashel. Cross the scenic Vee Gap through the Knockmealdown Mountains then potter around pretty Lismore village, dominated by a grey-stone castle.

DISTANCE: 122km (76 miles)
TIME: A full day
START: Waterford city
END: Lismore
POINTS TO NOTE: On Sundays, some sights and more individual shops in Waterford city may be closed. From Waterford to Cashel via Clonmel is 71km (44 miles). If you are driving to the southwest from Dublin, start the tour at Cashel. From Cashel to Lismore is 51km (32 miles). From Lismore you can return to Waterford (63km/39 miles) on the N72 and N25 or continue west on the N72 to Fermoy and N8 to Cork (49.5km/30 miles).

Waterford is the largest city in the southeast, but even then it only has a population of about 53,000. Founded by the Vikings between 853 and 914AD, it was the first settlement to be occupied by the Normans, who came from Wales in 1170. It owes its historic importance to its sheltered location on the mouth of the River Suir, and its relative proximity to the Welsh coast.

The rural counties of Waterford and Tipperary have rich fertile plains and small, quiet towns. The mighty Rock of Cashel, once home to the Kings of Munster, is a legacy of the area's wealth and strategic importance in pre-Christian and medieval times.

Waterford city

In its eighteenth-century heyday **Waterford** ❶ was an important port, and its long quays, though awaiting redevelopment, are still impressive. Quaint, cobbled streets alternate with gracefully proportioned Georgian buildings. The building of the largely pedestrianised shopping centre unearthed many treasures from its Viking and Norman past, now displayed in a fine museum.

The quays

Park on the quays, and if the weather is fine, stroll up towards the town clock along the once-busy cut-stone docks. Then head for the unmistakable

Waterford Crystal factory tour

pepper-pot bastion **Reginald's Tower** (www.waterfordtreasures. com, charge) at the quays' eastern extremity. This twelfth-century drum tower is 24 metres (80ft) tall and has been used as a mint, prison and military store. It is now restored and houses a collection of treasures that includes Viking and Norman artefacts unearthed in recent excavations. Highlights include a gold brooch from 1210AD, a sword given by Henry VIII to Waterford's Mayor in 1536, and eighteenth-century Irish silver. The ground floor is home to one of the town's most popular daytime eating spots, **The Granary**, see ❶.

Waterford Crystal Visitor Centre
Turn right out of Reginald's Tower and walk inland along the Mall to the headquarters of **Waterford Crystal** (www.waterfordvisitorcentre. com, charge). 'Old Waterford Glass', a heavy lead crystal produced between 1783 and 1851, is much sought-after by collectors for its outstanding light-refracting properties. The dramatic factory tour is as popular as ever so book in advance online to avoid queuing.

Rock of Cashel

Leave Waterford on the N24, heading west through **Carrick-on-**

Waterford Crystal chandeliers

Suir and **Clonmel 2**. The latter is a busy market town on the River Suir known for its apple orchards and cider-making. About 500 metres/yds west of Clonmel, take the R688 northwest to Cashel.

The **Rock of Cashel 3** (www.heritageireland.ie; charge), a 63-metre (206ft) limestone outcrop topped with ruined towers and gables, looms up suddenly from the flat plain. Its unexpected beauty causes a sharp intake of breath.

The Rock was originally a stronghold of the Kings of Munster who ruled southwest Ireland during the early Middle Ages. On converting to Christianity in 1101, King Muirchertach Ua Briain gave his fortress to the Church. Most of the buildings here date from the thirteenth to fifteenth centuries.

Exploring the Rock

After buying your ticket, turn right into the enclosure to avoid following the herd, then stroll around the northern perimeter, enjoying views of the plains of Tipperary. Note the high-up entrance at the base of the round tower, which made it a safe refuge.

Now walk through the roofless Gothic cathedral to the **Crossing**, a complex arch where two churches interlink. Turn left out of the cathedral to **Cormac's Chapel** (access by guided tour only from May–Sept

each year due to restoration work), one of Europe's finest examples of Hiberno-Romanesque architecture. Look up at the huge, rounded arches above each of the doors, and the ingenious curved roof.

Cashel town

It is only a few minutes' walk south (past an old chapel now converted into a fine-dining restaurant, **Chez Hans**, and an adjacent daytime café) to the centre of **Cashel**, a quiet country town with some old-fashioned wooden shop fronts. Turn south for the **Heritage Centre** (Main Street; www.cashel.ie, free), which has a display about the historical relationship between the town and the Rock, and a scale model of Cashel in the 1600s; it also contains the Tourist Information Office.

Vee Gap

Drive south on the N8, taking the R670 for **Cahir 4** and following it as it turns sharply right down a hill through the town. Cahir's most notable feature is its **castle** (www.heritageireland.ie, castle), a massive twelfth-century limestone fortress set on a rock in the River Suir.

The R668 turning to Clogheen is on the left immediately after the castle. As you drive towards Ballylooby, the **Knockmealdown Mountains** are straight ahead. Take a sharp left in **Clogheen** for the

Rock of Cashel

Vee Gap ⑤, a scenic mountain pass. The road curves around a peat-covered mountain, past a black corrie lake, to a height of 653 metres (2,144ft). Park here and look back across the flat plain of Tipperary to Cahir at the foot of the Galtee Mountains. Up here, there are no inhabitants (just sheep) and the vegetation is mainly grass and heather. Descending into the valley of the Blackwater River, the vegetation increases, with rhododendrons and a rich undergrowth of ferns.

Lismore

Continue south on the R688. As you cross the bridge into **Lismore** ⑥ you will have a dramatic view of **Lismore Castle**, perched on a cliff above the River Blackwater. This mid-nineteenth-century building is the Irish residence of the Duke of Devonshire; it is not open to the public. The village itself was home to a sixth-century monastery founded by St Carthage and was built to house the workers on the Duke's estates; during the famine years the people of Lismore suffered particularly badly.

Park and walk to the **Lismore Heritage Centre** (www.discover lismore.com, free). Formerly the town courthouse, the centre has a shop, tourist information, and a video presentation on the town's history.

Food and Drink

① The Granary Café
Hanover Street, Merchant's Quay, Waterford; www.granarycafe.ie
The self-service counter is packed with home-baked treats like lemon meringue pie or foccacia. There's a sheltered outdoor patio, and sofas and tables in the museum lobby. €

Village walk
Turn right and walk along Lismore's main street. Among the pleasant mix of shops and antiques stores are several pubs and restaurants. Turn left up the broad North Mall, which leads to **St Carthage's Cathedral** (daily 9.30am–5.30pm; free), a modest mid-seventeenth-century church in the neo-Gothic style with some interesting memorial stones from an earlier ninth-century church. Take the cobbled footpath to the left of the church leading downhill, and turn left at the main road to return to the car park.

Just here is the entrance to **Lismore Castle Gardens and Art Gallery** (www.lismorecastle. com, charge). The 3ha (7 acres) of gardens consist of woodland walks and contemporary sculpture, with good views of the castle. The gardens are also lovely and you can pre-order a picnic box online.

Tipperary from Vee Gap

Lismore Castle

WALK 6
Cork City and Harbour

After a walking tour of the centre of Cork city, including its bustling indoor food market and renowned art gallery, visit a thriving wildlife park, a classic shooting lodge surrounded by gardens and Cobh, formerly Queenstown, final departure point for the Titanic and many Irish emigrants in the nineteenth and twentieth centuries.

DISTANCE: City walk: 0.75km (0.5 miles); drive: 24.5km (15 miles)
TIME: 1 or 2 days
START: Cork city
END: Cobh
POINTS TO NOTE: Allow two days if you include a visit to the university. Note that Cork is busiest on Saturdays and quietest on Mondays. Many city attractions are closed on Sundays. Trains run to Fota and Cobh every half hour from Kent Station (Lower Glanmire Road; www.irishrail. ie), on the city's northern side. From Cork, you can head 30km (18 miles) south to Kinsale (tour 7), or west on the N22 to Killarney and the Ring of Kerry (tour 8) and Tralee and the Dingle Peninsula (tour 9).

Cork's city centre is built on an island formed by two channels of the River Lee. In the eighteenth and early nineteenth century cargoes of butter, beef and animal hides were exported from the city's many quays, creating a rich merchant class who built an attractive city of bridges and steeples. In the nineteenth century shipping moved downstream to the deep-water harbour at Cobh. The view of Cobh's steeply terraced houses beneath the soaring Gothic cathedral was the last, often tear-blurred, sight most emigrants had of their homeland.

The northern side of the city rises steeply from the river and wits like to joke that this is the origin of the distinctly 'up-and-down' Cork accent. You will hear fine examples of this on St Patrick Street in the afternoons, when newspaper sellers hawk the *Evening Echo* with loud cries of 'Eeeeeko'.

Cork city

Start at the **Tourist Information Office ❶** (T 021 425 5100; Mon–Sat 9am–5pm), located where Saint Patrick's Street meets the River Lee quays, near the famous Father Mathew Statue, commemorating the reforming priest. Directly ahead,

River view

was originally Cork's Custom House. The collection is strong on eighteenth–twenty-first-century British and Irish painting, stained glass and classical sculpture. There is a café with excellent fresh food.

Paul and St Patrick Streets

Continue into **Paul Street ❹**. This is Cork's 'left bank', with antiques shops, bookshops, art galleries, boutiques, cafés and buskers. Take a left along Carey's Lane and then a right into **St Patrick Street ❺**, a wide curved thoroughfare and the traditional place for a Saturday afternoon promenade.

English Market

Via Princes Street, enter the **English Market ❻** (www.englishmarket. ie), a Victorian covered market. Step back to view the imposing classical entrance. (It's worth looking up regularly in Cork to enjoy the ornate Victorian facades that often survive above the modern shop fronts.) A foodie-heaven, the market has about 150 stalls, from traditional butchers to purveyors of farmhouse cheeses and

at the northern extremity of Patrick Street, **St Patrick's Bridge ❷** spans the River Lee and leads to the steep northern side of Cork city.

Crawford Municipal Art Gallery

Stay on the southbank, however, and walk west along Lavitt's Quay until you reach the Opera House (built in 1965 and recently endowed with a stylish facade and a pedestrianised forecourt). Turn left on to Emmett Place for the **Crawford Municipal Art Gallery ❸** (Emmett Place; www.crawfordart gallery.ie, free), a large, Dutch-style red-brick building that dates from 1724. It

English Market

Kiss the Blarney

Blarney Castle (www.blarneycastle.ie), 10km (6 miles) northwest of Cork city, is still a must for first-time visitors. The building itself (one of Ireland's biggest tower houses) is impressive in bulk, although it is a roofless ruin, and you must climb a spiral of 84 stone steps (wear trainers) to reach the top. To kiss the famous Blarney Stone – in the hope of acquiring 'the gift of the gab' – you need to lie on your back and lean your head out over the castle's ramparts while being held securely by staff who handle some 300,000 stone-kissers a year. The fifteenth-century castle is situated in a landscaped park with a large lake and two rivers, and is surrounded by 'Druidic' rock gardens. The whole experience is presented tongue-in-cheek as a load of Blarney, but nevertheless makes a good half-day outing. Across the village green at Ireland's biggest craft shop, Blarney Woollen Mills (www.blarney.com), you can acquire a sweater and a woolly hat to complete your Irish initiation.

University College

To extend your city tour, hop on a bus (nos 205 or 208, which both stop along St Patrick Street) heading to **University College Cork ⑦** (Western Road; www.ucc.ie; visitor centre Mon–Fri 9am–5pm, Sat noon–5pm; free), home to some 15,000 students. Highlights here include the Tudor-Gothic-style quadrangle (1854), the Crawford Observatory (1878), the Hiberno-Romanesque-style Honan Chapel (1916), the Glucksman Gallery (2005), displaying contemporary art, and a superb collection of Ogham stones inscribed with the Celtic alphabet.

Cork Harbour

You can travel to Fota and Cobh either by rail or road. Note that the 25-minute train ride from Kent Station provides dramatic sea views that cannot be seen from a car. If you are driving, you should

hand-made chocolates – do not miss the alley of freshly landed seafood. Walking straight through the market will bring you to a piazza where **Farmgate Café** occupies an overhead balcony, see ❶. Closed Sundays.

Giraffes at Fota Wildlife Park

follow the N8 then the N22 east, turning off at the Fota and Cobh signpost after 10km (6 miles).

Fota Island

Fota Island ❽ and Cobh are both on the shores of Cork's outer harbour. The 47 ha (116-acre) estate of Fota House is surrounded by several kilometres of stone wall, and contains a golf course and luxury hotel. Go to the second entrance for **Fota Wildlife Park** (www.fotawildlife.ie, charge), which has giraffes, wallabies, ostriches, zebras and antelopes roaming free, plus a large enclosure for cheetahs. The car park also serves **Fota House, Gardens and Arboretum** (www.fotahouse.com, charge). The arboretum is over 200 years old and includes rhododendrons and azaleas (at their best in late spring). The Regency-style house was originally a shooting lodge; its servants' quarters retain many original features and there are impressive plaster ceilings in the ground-floor rooms.

Cobh

The road from Fota to **Cobh** ❾ (pronounced 'cove') skirts the edge of Cork Harbour for 6km (4 miles). About 1km (0.6 miles) beyond the cranes of an abandoned dockyard, look out for a signpost on the right to **Cobh Heritage Centre** (www.cobhheritage.com, free) and park beside it. If you are coming by train, the station is next to the Heritage Centre.

Food and Drink

❶ The Farmgate Café
English Market, Princes Street; www.farmgatecork.ie
A unique venue on a terrace above the English Market's bustle. All food is delicious and sourced in the market. €

The Centre occupies a Victorian railway station beside a deep-water berth once used by transatlantic liners. Cobh was the last port of call for the 'unsinkable' RMS *Titanic* in 1912, and also received survivors and the drowned from RMS *Lusitania*, sunk off this coast by a German submarine in 1915. At the time, the town was called Queenstown, having been renamed to celebrate the visit of Queen Victoria in 1849 (it reverted to Cobh in 1920). Within the Centre, **The Queenstown Story** is a lively audiovisual display about the town's seafaring past and Irish emigration.

From here, walk towards the town, an attractive south-facing Victorian resort. The seafront has a Victorian town park and opposite is the ***Lusitania Memorial***, dedicated to the 1,198 people who died when the ocean liner sank on 7 May 1915. Overhead is the tall spire of the neo-Gothic **St Colman's Cathedral**. Walk up to its entrance for a fine view of Cork Harbour and its islands, with the open sea beyond.

Colourful Cobh houses

TOUR 7
West Cork Coast

Spend a day exploring the rural coastline of west County Cork, starting in Kinsale, a historic port turned fashionable resort, then meandering along coastal roads and through quiet countryside to the sheltered waters and lush vegetation of Bantry Bay and Glengarriff.

DISTANCE: 136km (85 miles)
TIME: A full day
START: Charles Fort, Kinsale
END: Glengarriff
POINTS TO NOTE: A car is essential for this tour. At the end, either return to Kinsale on the R586 from Bantry (88km/54 miles) or push on 27km (17 miles) to Kenmare, or 80km (50 miles) to Killorglin, on the Ring of Kerry (tour 8).

Once a run-down rural backwater, west Cork coast's proximity to Cork Airport, its friendly people and its unspoilt environment have led many to buy holiday homes in the area, while others have relocated permanently, bringing prosperity to the region. This tour heads west, skirting rocky headlands.

Kinsale

Charles Fort

Approaching Kinsale from Cork, look out for a signpost to **Charles**

Charles Fort

Fort ❶ (www.heritageireland.ie, free), 2km (1.2 mile) outside town on the outer harbour. This massive star-shaped fort encloses 3ha (8 acres) of land and was built in 1680. In clear weather you can see the **Old Head of Kinsale**, the western extremity of the beautiful fjord-like harbour. Drive north along the coast road into town.

Kinsale Town

Kinsale ❷, 29km (18 miles) south of Cork city, overlooks the estuary of the Bandon River. Its narrow streets and tall Georgian houses are clustered around the sides of a conical hill. This now-fashionable resort, famous for its restaurants, is best known for the Battle of Kinsale (1601), in which the combined forces of the (Catholic) Irish and Spanish armies were defeated by the (Protestant) English. Afterwards, several important Irish clan chiefs – led by Hugh O'Neill of Ulster – fled to Europe in the 'Flight of the Earls', enabling the English to divide up their land into plantations, which they gifted to Protestants.

Park on the quay, walk up Pearse Street and then turn left then right for **Desmond Castle** (www.heritageireland.ie), a fifteenth-century tower house, which contains the **International Museum of Wine** celebrating the Irish families who took up winemaking after leaving for France in the seventeenth century (their names may be familiar: Hennessy, Barton, Lynch, Dillon). Unfortunately, in recent years the castle appears to be closed the public (despite the opening hours displayed on the website), but it's a beautiful sight even from the outside.

Taste test Kinsale's reputation for high-quality food by dining at **Bastion**, see ①.

The road to Skibbereen

The R600 crosses the River Bandon heading west to quieter country where a slow pace of life prevails. The road follows a wide sea inlet to

Timoleague ❸, a sleepy village where the ruins of a fourteenth-century **Franciscan friary** overlook the estuary.

Drombeg Stone Circle

To see more than a glimpse of **Clonakilty** ❹, a pretty market town with traditional wooden shop fronts and carefully tended floral displays, you'll need to pull off the N71. On the inlet at **Rosscarbery** ❺, flocks of swans glide by. About 200 metres/yds further on, take the R597 west (left) for Glandore. After about 5km (3 miles) a sign leads to **Drombeg Stone Circle** ❻, sited on a plateau facing the distant sea. This is one of the most complete examples of the region's mysterious early Bronze Age remains. A burial site, carbon-dated to 1124–794BC, was excavated at the centre of the ring of fourteen stones, but nobody knows who built the circle or what it signified to them. Locally,

Kinsale

it is believed to be in alignment with the setting sun at the winter solstice. Beside it is a Bronze Age cooking pit, with full instructions.

Millionaire's Row

Continue west to **Glandore** ❼, a line of south-facing houses perched on top of a cliff, nicknamed 'Millionaire's Row'. There is a magical view over a pair of islands to the open sea beyond. In sunny weather it is hard to resist an outdoor drink; try **Hayes' Bar**, see ❷.

Skibbereen

Follow the narrow road through Glandore along the wooded estuary, re-joining the N71 at **Leap**. Continue west to **Skibbereen** ❽, a small market town, once a major junction on the West Cork Railway. The tiny **Skibbereen Heritage Centre** (Upper Bridge Street; www.skibbheritage. com) explains the Great Famine of 1845–9, which took the lives of more than 100,000 people locally.

As it approaches **Ballydehob** ❾, a brightly painted hill village, the N71 turns inland and climbs across remote, sparsely inhabited hills, some planted with Sitka spruce, before winding down to gentler climes.

If you like lighthouses, detour 22.5km (14 miles) southwest from Ballydehob on the R592 to the **Mizen Head Signal Station Visitor Centre** (www.mizenhead.ie). The centre is in the lighthouse-keeper's house on an island at the tip of the rocky peninsula, accessed by a suspension bridge.

Bantry Bay

Bantry ❿, a quiet seaport and market town, is at the southeastern corner of the bay of the same name. The rafts that you see on the bay are evidence of the biggest local industry: mussel farming. You can sample the product in town at **O'Connor's Seafood Restaurant**, see ❸.

Bantry House and Garden (www.bantryhouse.com) is set on a height overlooking the 6km (4-mile) -wide bay and the serried ranks of surrounding mountains. The large mid-eighteenth-century mansion is well worth a visit. Its interior contains a fine selection of treasures brought back by the first Earl of Bantry from Europe in the early nineteenth century, and there is an extensive garden.

Glengarriff and Garinish Island

Beyond Bantry, the N71 runs along the water's edge through wooded **Ballylickey**, rising to a height above Bantry Bay, where there are several viewing points. Then it's downhill again to **Glengarriff** ⓫, a sheltered inlet at the top of the bay with a sub-tropical climate. The harbour here is presided over by the **Glengarriff Eccles Hotel**, see ❹.

Continue into the village and park near Quills Woollen Market. Beside the public toilets is a kiosk selling

Old Head of Kinsale

Food and Drink

❶ Bastion

Junction Market Street and Main Street,
Kinsale; www.bastionkinsale.com
Upmarket foodie heaven in a
smartly designed contemporary
restaurant. Tasting menus place
an imaginative spin on traditional
dishes, such as bacon and cabbage.
Wonderfully attentive service.
Reservations are required. €€€

❷ Hayes' Bar

The Square, Glandore;
www.hayesrestaurant.ie
This simple local has a superb bay
view and offers a surprising range
of wines by the glass. Local prawns,
crab and salmon are served in open
sandwiches and West Cork farmhouse
cheese features in the croque monsieur.
Open for lunch and dinner. €

❸ O'Connor's Seafood Restaurant

The Square, Bantry;
www.oconnorseafood.com
This superb town centre restaurant
offers up a shoal of seafood
delights, including chowder, oysters,
calamari, fresh lobster by the pound
and mussels prepared in three
different ways. Meat eaters and
vegetarians are catered for. €€€

❹ Glengarriff Eccles Hotel Restaurant

Glengarriff Harbour
www.eccleshotel.com
All kinds of notable writers have stayed
here, from William Thackeray to W.B.
Yeats to Virginia Woolf. The food is
standard hotel/bar fare, but you should
visit this large 250-year-old hotel
for its splendid location overlooking
Glengarriff Harbour and the atmosphere
of Victorian grandeur that persists. €€

tickets for **boat trips** from the Blue
Pool ferry point. Choose between
an hour-long **harbour trip**, with
close-up views of basking seals, or a
visit to **Garnish Island** (also known
as Illnacullin; www.garnishisland.
com, 10 minutes offshore. **Harbour
Queen Ferries** (www.harbourqueen
ferry.com, charge, runs every 30
mins Apr–Oct) provides a regular
service to the island from the Main
Pier in Glengarriff. In the early

twentieth century the 15ha (37
acres) of land on the island were
transformed into a series of formal
and informal gardens, using unusual
shrubs and rare subtropical flowers,
the whole framed by the rocky
peaks of the surrounding hills.

For a scenic walk, drive through
the busy village to **Glengarriff Woods
Nature Reserve** (www.glengarriff
naturereserve.ie, free), where there
are a number of way-marked trails.

Bantry House

TOUR 8
The Ring of Kerry

The Ring of Kerry is one of Europe's great scenic drives, a circular tour around the rim of the Iveragh Peninsula, through rugged sandstone hills and lush sub-tropical vegetation, with spectacular mountain and coastal views.

DISTANCE: 140km (87 miles)
TIME: 1 or 2 days
START: Killorglin
END: Kenmare
POINTS TO NOTE: A car is essential to tour the Ring independently. Tour bus traffic leaves Killarney 16km (10 miles) east of Killorglin between 9am and 10am travelling anti-clockwise, so leave earlier or later. If heavy rain is forecast, make other plans. Allow two days if you intend to visit the Skellig Rocks, a 3–4 hour boat trip; book ahead and bear in mind the ferry leaves Portmagee at 10am.

The Ring of Kerry follows the coast of the Iveragh Peninsula in the extreme southwest. The tour overlooks Dingle Bay to the north, the open Atlantic to the west and the sheltered waters of Kenmare Bay to the south. Inland, to the east, are the purple hills known as Macgillycuddy's Reeks and the Lakes of Killarney. The Gulf Stream ensures a mild, frost-free climate.

Dingle Bay

At **Killorglin** ❶ on the River Laune join the Ring of Kerry (N70) by driving west across the river and up the steep main street. This market town is known for Puck Fair (www.puckfair. ie), a street festival held every August.

Kerry Bog Village Museum

The scenery begins about 8km (5 miles) beyond Killorglin amid wild, sparsely inhabited hills. Stop at the **Red Fox Inn** for the **Kerry Bog Village Museum** ❷ (daily 9.30am–6pm), three reconstructed cottages with turf fires, ponies and dogs. It commemorates a simple rural lifestyle, which persisted until the mid-twentieth century.

Rossbeigh

Just beyond tiny **Glenbeigh**, detour 2km (1.25 miles) on the R564 to **Rossbeigh** ❸, a 6km (4-mile) sandy beach facing north across Dingle Bay. Take a few minutes to get your bearings and enjoy the sea air. After Glenbeigh the road curves dramatically towards the

Coastal view on the Ring of Kerry

coast, following a cliff top between the mountains and the pounding Atlantic.

Cahirsiveen

Cahirsiveen ❹ is the chief market town of south Kerry, but usually has a deserted air, even more than 150 years after being devastated by the Famine. Park near the **Tourist Information Office** (Church Street) and walk down the side road to the **Old Barracks** (www.theoldbarracks. net; charge), an exotic white-turreted building that once housed the local constabulary. Restored as a heritage centre, it has informative displays on local history, including the Famine. From here, you can see the estuary of the Carhen River, the more attractive side of town. Back at the main road turn west to the **O'Connell Memorial Church**, a huge Gothic-style edifice with

a black limestone facade, built in 1888.

Atlantic coast

As you leave Cahirsiveen, the **Valentia Observatory**, now part of the Irish meteorological service, is on the right. It was originally sited on Valentia Island in 1868, because the island had a telegraphic link to London and was in the path of most weather systems coming in from the Atlantic.

Portmagee and Skellig Rocks

Shortly beyond the observatory, head west for 12km (7.5 miles) to **Portmagee** ❺, a tiny fishing village and the departure point for the boat trip to Skellig Rocks. Go to where the Stars Wars actors hung out – scenes from both *Star Wars: The Force Awakens* (2015) and *Star Wars: The*

The Liberator

Daniel O'Connell (1775–1847), 'the Liberator', was born in Cahirsiveen and adopted by an uncle from whom he inherited an estate at Derrynane. Landowner, lawyer and orator, he dominated Irish politics in the early nineteenth century. Educated in France, he introduced genuine democracy to Ireland and was responsible for the Catholic Emancipation Act of 1829, allowing Catholics and Dissenters to vote, enter the professions and own land. Tall, burly and inexhaustible, O'Connell's immense appetite and physical stamina were legendary. He was no saint; he fought a fatal duel in his youth and had a reputation as a womaniser. Most Irish towns and villages have an O'Connell Street, including Dublin.

Sneem

its dry-stone buildings clinging dramatically to the cliff-edge, as they have done since the seventh century.

If you are unable to take the boat trip, drive across the causeway to **Valentia Island** to visit the **Skellig Experience Visitor Centre** ❼ (www.skelligexperience.com; opening hours vary, check website for details), which introduces the UNESCO-listed Skellig Michael and the other rocks.

Last Jedi (2017) were filmed on Skellig Michael – at **The Bridge Bar**, see ❶.

Weather permitting, small open boats make the 13km (8-mile) crossing from Portmagee to **Skellig Rocks** ❻ (www.skelligexperience.com/other-sea-tours; boats depart 9–10.30am and return 2–3pm) in about an hour. **Little Skellig** is home to over 27,000 gannets, while **Skellig Michael** (where landing is permitted) rises to a double peak 217 metres (712ft) high. More than five hundred stone steps lead to a simple monastery,

Waterville

Return to the main Ring road and drive south 11km (7 miles) to **Waterville** ❽, a small resort famous for its golf course and the game angling on Lough Currane. Park in the centre near the Butler Arms and statue of Charlie Chaplin, who used to holiday here, and take a walk on the windswept sandy beach.

Lough Leane, Killarney

Killarney

Killarney National Park (www.killarney nationalpark.ie, free) is a car-free zone and Muckross Park is at its core. Hire a jaunting car (open horse-drawn carriage, charge) at the park gates: the park has wild deer, walking trails, a lakeside manor and Muckross Traditional Farms (www.muckross-house.ie, charge), a beguiling outdoor museum of rural life.

For a quintessential Killarney experience, take a half-day Gap of Dunloe tour (O'Connor Autotours, Ross Road, Killarney; www.oconnorauto tours.ie; May–Oct), which proceed on a pony and trap or on foot through 6km (4 miles) of narrow, unpaved mountain passes past huge glacial boulders, returning to town by boat. End the day by watching the sun set over the lakes from the seventh-century monastic ruins at Aghadoe. Killarney's Tourist Information Office is on Beech Road.

Derrynane House

Stop at the parking area on the **Coomakista Pass** ❾ to enjoy views of the Skelligs to the west and the mountains of the Beara Peninsula to the south.

In **Caherdaniel** drive downhill to **Derrynane House and National Park** ❿ (www.derrynanehouse.ie, charge) family home of Daniel O'Connell. The modest 1702 manor house is

Food and Drink

❶ The Bridge Bar
Portmagee; www.moorings.ie
The simply prepared fish is leaping fresh; alternatively, opt for the roast of the day. €

furnished with heirlooms. Walk along the beach and explore the rock pools.

Kenmare River

The Kenmare River is a sea inlet that divides the Iveragh Peninsula from the Beara Peninsula in the south.

Sneem

Brightly painted **Sneem** has two village greens; park by the second. Walk down the road beyond the Blue Bull (signposted 'Pier') for about 300 metres/yds. Looking back through the reeds you can appreciate Sneem's sheltered location between the sea and the hills. Note the difference in vegetation on this side of the Ring; in the place of bare windswept rocks is a lush growth of trees and shrubs.

Kenmare

Follow the N70 east for 27km (17 miles) to **Kenmare** ⓬. Laid out in 1755 in a compact triangle, it is packed with restaurants and shops. Park in its centre beside the green and the **Kenmare Heritage Centre**.

Ladies' View, Killarney　　　Muckross Traditional Farms

TOUR 9
The Dingle Peninsula

Jutting out into the Atlantic, the Dingle Peninsula is Europe's most westerly point. The Irish-speaking area at its tip is rich in prehistoric and early Christian remains and features rugged cliffs and fine sandy beaches. Finish by crossing the jaw-dropping Conor Pass towards Tralee in Kerry.

DISTANCE: 125km (77.5 miles)
TIME: A full day
START: Castlemaine
END: Tralee
POINTS TO NOTE: There is a daily Bus Éireann service from Tralee to Dingle town (no. 275), but really a car is essential for this tour. Avoid the Conor Pass in misty weather; take the N86 from Dingle all the way to Tralee.

Begin at Castlemaine, the southern gateway to the Dingle Peninsula (Corca Dhuibhne), which stretches for some 48km (30 miles) from Tralee in the east to Slea Head in the west.

Castlemaine to Dingle

Some 10km (6 miles) beyond **Castlemaine ①**, the sea comes into view as the road skirts Castlemaine Harbour. The first hint of the scenery to come is at **Inch ②**, where a 6km (4-mile) -long sand spit backed by dunes stretches out into Dingle

Bay. Stop for a swim, surf or walk along the unusual west-facing beach and refuel at **Sammy's**, see ❶.

Annascaul

The wide road at **Annascaul ③**, where the Castlemaine and Tralee roads meet, was once the location of a major cattle fair, which is also why this tiny village has so many pubs. One such pub, the **South Pole Inn** (www.southpoleinn.com) was built by Tom Crean (1877–1938), a local man of legendary strength who enlisted in the Royal Navy and served on three Antarctic expeditions, with both Scott and Shackleton. The pub is crammed with fascinating memorabilia, and you can enjoy a view of green hills and grazing sheep from its front door.

Dingle town and harbour

From Annascaul, it's 17km (10.5 miles) west to **Dingle ④** (An Daingean). Turn left at the entrance and park on the pier. Dingle has a population of about 1,500, which can

Dingle harbour

treble in summer. Its fame was spread by the filming of *Ryan's Daughter* in 1969, and again in 1983 by the arrival of a dolphin, Fungie who attracted visitors in their droves. Although long gone, his legacy in the town's tourist trade lives on and a bronze statue on the pier stands proudly in his honor. Opposite, in a humble tin shed, is one of Dingle's best seafood restaurants, **Out of the Blue**, see ➋.

A triangular 10-minute walk from the pier up Green Street, down Main Street and back along the Mall will take you past most of the town's shops and restaurants. While on Main Street, try the chowder and a pint of creamy stout at **Ashe's Seafood Restaurant & Bar**, see ➌. The better craft shops are at the top of Green Street.

Slea Head drive

Head west for 6km (4 miles) on the R559 to **Ventry** ➎ (Ceann Trá), an Irish-speaking village with a few pubs and shops. The bay here offers a long sandy beach and safe swimming.

Between Ventry and Slea Head there are over four hundred small conical huts of un-mortared stone known as beehive huts. While some date from the fifth to eighth centuries and were used by hermit monks, many were built in the early twentieth century to house farm implements; timber is so scarce here that it is cheaper to build with stone.

Dunbeg Fort

About 6km (4 miles) further, stop at the distinctive Stone House Restaurant at **Fahan** to visit **Dunbeg Promontory Fort** (charge), a defensive promontory fort that was inhabited during about 800–1200AD. A short film introduces the compact site, which has an inner drystone rampart and a souterrain. It is perched right on the cliff's edge (and is in danger of falling in), reached by a short downhill path beside a field grazed by donkeys. About 250 metres/yds on, park again to visit a group of **beehive huts** above the road. In fine weather you can look south across the sea to the Skellig Rocks, where hardy monks lived in similar shelters.

Slea Head

The road climbs west around Eagle Mountain to **Slea Head** ❻ (Ceann Sléibhe), marked by a life-size roadside Crucifixion. **Coumenole**, the sandy beach below, will be familiar from *Ryan's Daughter*. The sea may look inviting, but swimming here is dangerous.

Dunquin and the Blasket Islands

Nearby **Dunquin** ❼ (Dún Chaoin) is a scattered settlement, as was the tradition in old Gaelic Ireland. The **Great Blasket** (An Blascaod Mór) is the largest of seven islands visible offshore. It was inhabited until 1953 by a tough, self-sufficient community of farmers and fishermen. The **Blasket Centre** (www.blasket.ie, charge) at Dunquin explains the islanders' heritage. From **Dunquin Pier** you can catch a ferry to the island with **Blasket Island Ferries** (www.blasketisland.com, charge, best to book in advance).

Gallarus Oratory

Continue on the R559 for 7km (4.25 miles) to Irish-speaking **Ballyferriter** ❽ (Baile an Fheirtéaraigh), the largest village (two shops and four pubs that serve simple food) on this side of the peninsula, founded by the Norman Ferriter family in the twelfth century and popular today with holidaymakers and Irish-language enthusiasts.

Some 8km (5 miles) further on is the **Gallarus Oratory** ❾ (www.gallarusoratory.ie, charge). This extraordinary eighth-century building of un-mortared stone is shaped like an inverted boat, and remains as dry and solid as the day it was built.

At the crossroads north of Gallarus, turn right (east) for the ruined **Kilmalkedar Church** ❿. It was built around 1150, although the settlement dates from the seventh century. The superbly carved Romanesque features have hardly weathered over the years. There are a number of interesting standing stones nearby, including a sundial stone and several Ogham stones, carved with letters from an early medieval alphabet.

Conor Pass to Tralee

Return to Dingle on the R559 (8km/5 miles). If the weather is fine, drive to Tralee (48km/30 miles) via the **Conor Pass** ⓫, a rocky mountain road that crosses the peninsula from south to north. It rises steeply to 456 metres (1,496ft) above sea level, and parts are so narrow that you must negotiate right of way with oncoming traffic. It is not for the faint-hearted, but it does offer spectacular vistas of

Slea Head

Brandon Bay and the wide Atlantic Ocean in the north; stop in a lay-by to enjoy the view. The road then corkscrews down to the bay, past a dazzling waterfall and boulder-strewn hillsides studded with glittering lakes.

Blennerville

There are glimpses of the sea as you drive along the R560 and join the N86 at **Camp**. Further on, **Blennerville** ⓬ is a mainly Georgian village perched between Tralee Bay and the old ship canal. It still has a large working windmill, best viewed from a distance.

Tralee

County town of Kerry, **Tralee** ⓭ (Trá Lí) has a population of more than 35,000, many of whom are students. Park in the centre near the town park beside **Ashe Memorial Hall**, an imposing neoclassical building housing the **Tourist Information Office**. The front entrance leads to the **Kerry County Museum** (www.kerrymuseum.ie; charge), with a lively display of Kerry's history from ancient times. Denny Street leads from the museum to the centre and contains the best of Tralee's Georgian architecture, mostly now lawyers' offices. A pedestrian alley on the left of Denny Street leads to Tralee's pedestrian piazza, which usually has a few market stalls trading. If you are in need of refreshment, try **The Grand Hotel**, see ❹, back on Denny Street.

Food and Drink

❶ Sammy's Café

Inch Beach; http://sammysinch.com
This café-bar has an amazing beach location. By day it serves fresh salads, burgers, soups and sandwiches; at night it's fish and steaks. €

❷ Out of the Blue

The Pier, Dingle town; www.outoftheblue.ie
It's a basic brightly painted shack with a hole in the wall beside the pier, but it serves the freshest of seafood cooked to perfection. Book in advance. €€€

❸ Ashe's Bar & Restaurant

Main Street, Dingle town; www.ashesrestaurant.ie
A traditional pub that began life as a drapery and general store and evolved into a great pub-restaurant serving legendary seafood chowder, local mussels, beef-and-Guinness stew. Family-owned for over 165 years. €€

❹ The Grand Hotel

Denny Street, Tralee; www.grandhoteltralee.com
This fine institution has an imposing Victorian facade. In the Pikeman's Bar there are good-value specials like roast leg of lamb and sea trout fillet. A more formal evening menu is served in Samuel's Restaurant. €€

Ventry Bay

TOUR 10
Limerick and Shannon

On this tour, explore the charming village of Adare, wander the medieval streets of Limerick and then head into the castle country around the Shannon estuary to discover more of Ireland's past at Bunratty Castle and Folk Park.

DISTANCE: 71km (44 miles)
TIME: A full day
START: Adare
END: Quin
POINTS TO NOTE: Adare is on the N21, 7km (4.25 miles) west of the N20 Cork–Limerick road and 17km (10 miles) southwest of Limerick city. From Quin, return to the N18, where you can head south for Limerick (34km/21 miles) or north for Lahinch (38km/23 miles), the starting point of tour 11.

The Limerick region and the Shannon estuary have been of great strategic importance ever since the Vikings established a sheltered seaport on an island at the head of the Shannon estuary in the ninth century, which grew into the city of Limerick. During the twelfth to fifteenth centuries, several monastic orders settled in the area, while Irish clan chieftains built fortified homes among the low hills and lakes to the northwest of Limerick. This castle country is dotted with the ruins of tower houses, some of which have been restored, such as Craggaunowen and magnificent Bunratty Castle.

Adare

Begin the day to the southwest of Limerick city at **Adare** ❶, which boasts of being 'Ireland's prettiest village'. It's a tiny place and you cannot miss the **Adare Heritage Centre** (Main Street; www.adareheritagecentre. ie, charge to visit the castle) at its heart. There is a large car park behind the centre, plus several crafts shops and a restaurant within. You can pick up a map of the village here.

Main Street

Turn left out of the Heritage Centre to the former **Trinitarian priory**, founded in 1230; it was converted into a Catholic parish church in 1811. The opposite side of the wide main street is lined by thatched cottages with flower-filled front gardens. They were built in 1830 by the local landlord, the Earl of Dunraven, for his workers. Today, most of them are either restaurants or craft shops.

Thatched cottage, Adare

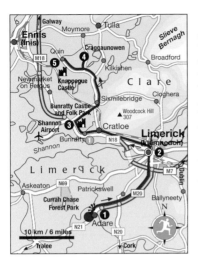

Lucy Erridge's (www.lucyerridge.com) is the most interesting of the latter.

Augustinian friary

Turn left out of the Dunraven Arms, which marks the end of the village, and continue for about 50 metres/ yds to the former **Augustinian friary**, now Adare's Anglican church. To the north of the church are the well-preserved cloisters of the 1315 monastery. The church's nave and choir also date from the fourteenth century.

The main gates of **Adare Manor** (www.adaremanor.com) are across the road from the church. The manor, which was enlarged in the Tudor Revival style in the mid-nineteenth century, is now a luxury hotel and golf resort.

River walk

At this point you could go through the metal stile beside the Anglican church for a lovely rural riverside walk of about 1.5km (1 mile). The walk follows the banks of the River Maigue, rich in wildlife, to the west, before looping back to the village centre down Station Road.

Limerick city

Leaving Adare for **Limerick** ❷ takes you out of a cosy time warp and into modern Ireland, with a dual carriageway (N20) approaching the Republic's third largest city. The bulk of the low-lying city is positioned on the eastern bank of the River Shannon (Ireland's longest river), and the wide, fast-flowing waterway is its best asset.

Follow signs for the centre. The **Limerick Tourist Information Office** (20 O'Connell Street; www.limerick. ie) is located on O'Connell Street. Good parking can be found nearby in the Arthur's Quay Centre. From the quay itself, where our walk begins, you can look along the banks of the broad majestic Shannon to King John's Castle.

Hunt Museum

Turn right up Francis Street and left into Rutland Street for the **Hunt Museum** ❹ (www.huntmuseum.com, charge). Once the city's Custom House, the compact Georgian building has the finest collection of Celtic and medieval treasures outside Dublin's National

Idyllic Adare

Augustinian friary, Adare

Museum, plus a small selection of Irish and European paintings, including works by Renoir and Picasso. Once a private collection, it was donated to the nation in 1976 by the Hunt family. There's also a shop and an excellent café overlooking the river.

St Mary's Cathedral

Turn left upon leaving the Hunt Museum and cross a bridge over a tributary of the Shannon to **King's Island**, site of the city's original settlement. On the left is **St Mary's Cathedral B** (www.saintmarys cathedral.ie; free, Sun services only). The rounded Romanesque entrance door is a remnant of its origins as a twelfth-century palace belonging to Donal Mór O'Brien, King of Munster. Much of the compact cruciform building dates from the fifteenth century, such as the black-oak misericords with carved animal features in the choir stalls. Visits Monday to Friday only.

King John's Castle

From the cathedral turn onto Nicholas Street and walk north for **King John's Castle C** (www.kingjohnscastle.com, charge) a massive fortification with curtain walls and two drum towers, built by the Normans in the 1200s and rebuilt and extended many times over the years. The outdoor courtyard gives access to the massive bastions and views of the river and city. The visitor centre

features exhibitions that bring to life the castle's dramatic history through twenty-first-century technology.

Riverside footpath

Turn right out of the castle, and right again down a pedestrian alley beside the castle walls, past the **Limerick Museum** (www.museum. limerick.ie, free), to return to the car park along a riverside footpath. At Merchant's Quay look for the modern white footbridge across the river.

King John's Castle, Limerick

North of Limerick city

Cross the River Shannon in County Clare via the N18, the road to Shannon Airport and the west of Ireland.

Bunratty Castle and Folk Park

Impressively big, **Bunratty Castle** ❸ (www.bunrattycastle.ie, charge) has a square tower at each corner and a drawbridge. Dating largely from the sixteenth century, it contains furniture and tapestries from the fourteenth to seventeenth centuries. In the evening Bunratty hosts 'medieval banquets' – a meal with Irish cabaret and plenty of 'Blarney'.

The extensive **Folk Park** (last entry 4.30pm) consists of 10ha (25 acres) of reconstructed traditional dwellings, including a typical village street c.1880, complete with pecking hens. The original inspiration for many an Irish theme pub, **Durty Nelly's** (www.durtynellys.ie) squats on the riverbank beside the castle. It does not serve food in the daytime, so turn right out of Bunratty Castle and after a short way you will see **J.P. Clarke's Country Pub**, see ❶.

Craggaunowen – the Living Past Experience

Take the narrow country lane behind J.P. Clarke's to the T-junction with the R471 and turn right for **Sixmilebridge**. Drive through the village and turn left onto the R469 for Craggaunowen, well signposted about 10km (6

miles) from Bunratty. Among the attractions at **Craggaunowen – the Living Past Experience** ❹ (www.craggaunowen.ie) are a restored 1550 castle and a reconstructed *crannóg*, a fortified dwelling of clay and wattle built on a lake island.

Quin

Retrace your steps from Craggaunowen and turn west onto the R469 for about 4km (2.5 miles), passing **Knappogue Castle** (www.knappoguecastle.ie, open seasonally, charge) built in 1467, en route to **Quin** ❺. In the village centre are the well-preserved remains of a **Franciscan abbey**, founded in 1402, with cloisters and elaborate stone tombs. Across the stream are the ruins of a thirteenth-century church. Drive across the bridge, and take the first left for about 5km (3 miles) to an interchange with the N18.

TOUR 10 NORTH OF LIMERICK CITY

Food and Drink

❶ J.P. Clarke's Country Pub
Bunratty; www.gallaghersof
bunratty.com
Escape the tour-bus trade at this stylish, modern pub close to the castle. The attractive high-ceilinged bar has an open fire and restaurant-style tables. The contemporary menu is strong on seafood; or try the burger with roast-pepper relish. €

St Mary's Cathedral doorway   Hunt Museum

TOUR 11
The Cliffs of Moher and the Burren

Drive along County Clare's attractive coast to the dramatic Cliffs of Moher, which rise vertically from the Atlantic, and the eerie Burren, a treeless limestone plateau that fascinates botanists, geologists and archaeologists.

DISTANCE: 78km (48.5 miles)
TIME: A full day
START: Lahinch
END: Kinvara
POINTS TO NOTE: Lahinch is also spelt Lehinch. It is 30km (18.5 miles) west of Ennis on the N85. Kinvara is 10km (6 miles) west of the N18 Galway–Limerick road and 30km (19 miles) south of Galway city (tour 12).

Lahinch, on the west coast of County Clare, has long been famous for its golf links and is now also one of Ireland's most popular surfing destinations. The huge bulk of the Cliffs of Moher rise 200 metres (650ft) straight out of the sea on this coast and stretch for some 7km (4.25 miles), offering distant views of the Aran Islands and close-up ones of nesting seabirds. To the north, the Burren is a National Park covering 500 sq km (200 sq miles) of lunar-like limestone pavement, with unique flora and fauna and numerous megalithic remains, dating from the Stone Age and the Bronze Age, long before the arrival of the Celts.

Lahinch to Liscannor

The driving tour begins with a right turn just before **Lahinch** ❶ (approaching from Ennis), but first carry straight on, turning right off the main road at the top of the village to park above the long sandy beach, where you can take a walk along its promenade. These days surfers may even outnumber golfers, and the village has a lively nightlife.

Return to the R478. The road curves north to west through the golf links and a series of sand dunes, with intermittent sea views.

Liscannor

The tiny village of **Liscannor** ❷ nearby is somewhat overwhelmed by newly built holiday homes, but still has an excellent pub at its centre, **Vaughan's Anchor Inn**, see ❶. The village has given its name to a black stone, Liscannor slate, usually used as flagstones, which bear the

The Cliffs of Moher

a bird's-eye view. In good weather, harpists and other buskers entertain outside. Note the extensive use of the local Liscannor stone as paving and seating.

The cliffs

Part of the recent investment in the Cliffs of Moher went on an upgrade of over 600 metres/yds of pathways and viewing platforms to enable visitors to enjoy the spectacle safely and without harming the area's wildlife and ecological balance. The natural layering of the rocks creates ledges that are an ideal habitat for nesting seabirds, including fulmars, kittiwakes, razorbills and puffins. The breeding season runs from May to July. For the full windswept experience, go right up to the edge and watch the waves booming far below. In clear weather you can see the Aran Islands and the far side of Liscannor Bay.

fossil remains of marine animals that lived up to 300 million years ago. In the early twentieth century, more than five hundred men were employed in local quarries.

As you head to the Cliffs of Moher, look out for **The Rock Shop** (www.therockshop.ie), which has interesting audio-visual displays about quarrying and a collection of antique tools, plus a nice tearoom.

The Cliffs of Moher

The exhilarating **Cliffs of Moher ❸** attract over a million visitors a year. Park at the multi-million-euro **Visitor Centre**, which is built into the hillside and roofed with grass. It contains a shop, ATM and café, plus **The Cliffs Exhibition**, the highlight of which is a virtual reality tour of the cliffs from

The Burren

The road now winds through the heart of the Burren, an evocative area defined by a surreal treeless plateau with swirling limestone terraces, huge rocks erratically deposited in the Ice Age and relics of prehistoric man, including cairns, court graves, dolmens

The Burren Way

The Burren Way runs from Ballyvaughan to Liscannor, a distance of 45km (26.5 miles). The terrain varies from rocky ground where only scrub grows to magnificent wide 'green paths', and is largely off-road. Part of the tour runs along the top of the Cliffs of Moher, with great views of the Aran Islands. As well as a wealth of wildflowers, you might well glimpse some of the Burren fauna, which includes wild goats, foxes, hares, rabbits, badgers, the rare pine marten (martes martes) and a rich diversity of butterfly species.

and more than 400 stone forts. The land once had a thin covering of soil, but time, weather and the farming activities of prehistoric man denuded the surface, leaving the lunar-like region seen today. Meanwhile, under the ground, acid in the rainwater has seeped through the limestone to create pools and caves. Some 125 types of plant from Alpine, Arctic and Mediterranean zones flourish here, often growing up through the rock; they are at their best in May.

Kilfenora

The R478 crosses the N67 outside Lisdoonvarna and becomes the R476, continuing for 9km (5.5 miles) to another tiny village, **Kilfenora ❹**.

Here, **St Fachtnan's Cathedral** is an attractive little 12th-century church with some finely carved effigies and three medieval high crosses. Next door, **The Burren Centre** (www.theburrencentre. ie) has a short film introducing the unique landscape of the Burren.

Leamaneh Castle

Continuing east, the left turn onto the R480 has an unmissable landmark, the beautifully proportioned ruins of **Leamaneh Castle ❺**. It is not open to the public and the surrounding lands are grazed by cattle. Close up, you can see that it was built in two phases: the tower in 1480 and the manor in 1640.

Poulnabrone Dolmen

The road between here and Ballyvaughan abounds in megalithic remains. A stone-walled car park has been built to accommodate visitors at the **Poulnabrone Dolmen ❻**, a structure over 3 metres (10ft) high and the Burren's finest portal tomb, dating back to 2500BC.

Aillwee Caves

The road then winds downhill through a series of corkscrew bends, with distant sea views, to **Aillwee Caves ❼** (www.aillweecave.ie). Fronted by a massive shop and flanked by a separate birds of prey attraction, this is one of the few Burren caves accessible

Cracked limestone of the Burren

to the public. The guided tour takes you about 300 metres/yds through narrow passages into chambers with vast stalactites and past waterfalls.

Around Galway Bay

The road skirts the southern shore of Galway Bay, a sheltered, indented coastline, and in good weather there are views of the purple hills of Connemara on the opposite shore.

Ballyvaughan

A small fishing village on the southern shore of Galway Bay with plenty of accommodation, **Ballyvaughan** ❽ is the starting point of the **Burren Way** way-marked walk, and a popular base for walkers and scholarly visitors to the **National Park** (www.burrennationalpark. ie) on the southeastern side of the Burren. **Monk's Bar**, see ❷, is a waterside bar with good food.

Kinvara

The road east out of Ballyvaughan skirts the shore of Galway Bay, and to the right offers stunning views of the grey, rocky heights of the Burren. **Kinvara** ❾, 20km (12 miles) east, at the top of the sheltered inlet of **Kinvara Bay**, is the kind of quiet fishing village that can steal your heart away. Turn left down the road beside the Merriman Hotel and right along its harbour to see it at its best. Kinvara is also known for the traditional music

> ## Food and Drink
>
> ### ❶ Vaughan's Anchor Inn
> Liscannor; www.vaughans.ie
> A reassuring aroma of fresh seafood greets you on opening the door; this traditional family-run pub is famed for its seafood, which is landed daily at the village pier. It's a child-friendly establishment, festooned with nautical bric-a-brac, with plentiful tables outside. €
>
> ### ❷ Monk's Bar
> Ballyvaughan; www.monks.ie
> Situated on the village's pier, from the outside there is an unforgettable view across Galway Bay. Inside, an open fire warms the long, low-ceilinged room, and there's a menu of soups, sandwiches, steaks, vegetarian stir-fry dishes and seafood specials. €

played in the pubs, such as **Green's Bar** (www.greensofkinvara.com).

Dunguaire Castle

Magnificently sited on a rock, **Dunguaire Castle** (www.dunguaire castle.com, charge) looks out to sea on the northern side of Kinvara Bay. Built in 1520, it has been fully restored, and hosts medieval banquets in the evening (Apr– Oct, charge, book in advance).

Dunguaire Castle

WALK 12
Galway

A half-day walk around the medieval centre of Galway, the main urban hub of the west of Ireland and a vibrant fast-growing city with a young population and distinctive Irish identity.

> **DISTANCE:** About 1km (0.6 mile)
> **TIME:** A half day
> **START/END:** Eyre Square
> **POINTS TO NOTE:** Galway city is 27km (17 miles) southeast of Oughterard, the starting point of tour 13, on the N59.

Galway city is situated where the River Corrib flows into the Atlantic Ocean. Its commercial centre is compact, largely pedestrianised and packed with quaint shops, trendy boutiques, stylish cafés and lively pubs.

Galway escaped the attention of the Vikings, thus retaining its Irish customs until the Anglo-Norman invasion in the thirteenth century. The invaders built a walled town, which developed as a thriving port. They traded in wine, spices and fish, forging strong links with Spain, rather than England and Wales, due to the town's westerly location. It became known as 'the City of the Tribes', as fourteen powerful Anglo-Norman merchant families controlled its wealth for many

centuries. Remnants of their stone-built mansions can still be seen in the city's narrow lanes and cobbled streets.

Eyre Square to the River Corrib

Begin at **Eyre Square** ❶, site of the **J.F. Kennedy Park** and the city's focal point. In the northern corner fourteen flags, each representing one of the merchant tribes, stand alongside the **Quincentennial Fountain** ❷, erected in 1984 to mark Galway's 500th anniversary as a city. Its rust-coloured 'sails' depict those of the Galway hooker, a traditional wooden cargo boat. The **Tourist Information Office** (091-537 700) is in Forster Street, off the eastern corner.

The northwestern side of Eyre Square leads into **Williamsgate Street** (look for the landmark **Brown Thomas** department store; www.brownthomas.com). This street is the spine of old Galway and changes its name four times before reaching the River Corrib.

Lynch's Castle

At the junction of William Street and Shop Street, the Allied Irish

Flags in Eyre Square

cathedral. There is a popular belief that Christopher Columbus prayed here in 1477 before setting off to discover America. The area around the church has a vibrant Saturday market.

A signpost will direct you to Bowling Green and the **Nora Barnacle House 5**, Ireland's smallest museum and family home of James Joyce's wife.

Quay Street

Return to the central spine via Lombard Street. On the corner of

Bank occupies one of Galway's oldest buildings, **Lynch's Castle 3**, a fifteenth-century fortified townhouse. Note the cheeky gargoyles, Lynch family arms and the carved stone panels on its facade. Inside, a 1651 map shows Galway's street layout, little changed today.

Collegiate Church of St Nicholas

Continue south and follow the next fork to the right, leading to the **Collegiate Church of St Nicholas 4**, founded in 1320 and now the Church of Ireland (Episcopalian)

Cross Street and Quay Street is **Tigh Neachtain 6** (Noctan's, www.tigh neachtain.com), one of Galway's most loved traditional pubs, with a warren-like wood-clad interior. It is also the unofficial information point for the city's busy arts scene.

To the left, on High Street, look for a sign to the pretty **Old Malte Mall**. To the right, on Quay Street, traditional shops selling tweeds and Aran sweaters prosper alongside vintage and designer clothing boutiques and contemporary arts-and-crafts galleries, a scene

Market near Church of St Nicholas

Aran Islands

The Aran Islands – Inishmore (Inis Mór), Inishman (Inis Meain) and Inisheer (Inis Oirr) – are strung across the mouth of Galway Bay. They contain many archaeological remains; the biggest is Inishmore's Dun Aengus (Dún Aoinghusa), a 2000 -year-old Celtic fort perched on a 90-metre (300ft) sheer cliff. The islands' wildlife is unusually rich, and walkers will enjoy the Atlantic air and narrow paths that run between tiny fields. Inishmore is the most popular; go to Inishman or Inisheer for solitude. Irish is the islanders' first language, but all speak English too.

Wait until arrival to book, so you can vary your plans according to the weather. Ferries from Rossaveal take an hour and there are bus connections to Galway city. Aran Island Ferries (www.aranislandferries. com) has daily sailings (€30 return). Aer Arann (www.aerarannislands.ie) operates daily flights year-round from Connemara Regional Airport in Inverin (from €35 one way). Shop around for deals including bed and breakfast; if possible, spend at least a night on an island for the full experience.

Food and Drink

1 McDonagh's Seafood House
22 Quay Street; www.mcdonaghs.net
A self-service chippy on one side and a seafood restaurant on the other, McDonagh's is a Galway institution. The chippy also offers a more elaborate menu than the usual takeaway fare with seafood chowder and a selection of seafood salads. €€

Along the Corrib

Quay Street reaches the Corrib at the open space of Spanish Parade. Turn left for the **Spanish Arch 7**, named after the city's former trading partner. Beside is the modern **Galway City Museum 8** (www.galwaycitymuseum.ie, free). Large flocks of swans congregate here, and there are usually a few Galway hookers moored on the opposite bank.

Riverside walk

Cross the road at Wolfe Tone Bridge and follow the footpath along this side of the river, past the William O'Brien Bridge all the way to the **Salmon Weir Bridge 9**. From mid-April to early July, you can spot shoals of salmon lying in the water before making their way upstream to Lough Corrib to spawn. Cross the bridge to visit the twentieth-century **Catholic Cathedral** before crossing back and taking the second right onto St Francis Street and leads towards Eyre Square.

enlivened by an international array of buskers. Most bars and restaurants here, including **McDonagh's**, see 1, have outside tables.

Quayside houses in Galway

TOUR 13
Connemara

Drive across sparsely inhabited, lake-studded bogland, with huge skies above, mountains ahead and hospitable villages en route. Highlights include the attractive town of Clifden, Connemara National Park, the romantic nineteenth-century Kylemore Abbey and the deep-water fjord at Killary Harbour.

DISTANCE: 86km (53.5 miles)
TIME: A full day
START: Oughterard
END: Leenane
POINTS TO NOTE: Oughterard is 27km (17 miles) west of Galway on the N59 Clifden road. Leenane is also on the N59, 32km (20 miles) south of Westport, the starting point of tour 14.

Stretching from Galway Bay in the south to Killary Harbour in the north, bordered by a rocky coastline and consisting mainly of rugged hills, windswept bogs and innumerable lakes, Connemara has always been an isolated place. Oscar Wilde described it as a 'savage beauty', and it remains relatively untamed. Its southern coast is home to Ireland's largest Gaeltacht (Irish-speaking area), while in north and central Connemara (covered by this tour) there are still more sheep than people; traditionally, people lived by the sea

where subsistence farming could be augmented by fishing. The central area has largely escaped unsightly new developments, while existing attractions have been quietly enhanced.

Lough Corrib

Oughterard ❶ (pronounced 'ookterard'), a village about 40 minutes' drive from Galway, grew up chiefly to accommodate anglers heading for Lough Corrib and consists largely of tackle shops, souvenir shops and small hotels. To orient yourself, on arriving in Oughterard turn right at the petrol station for a 1km (0.6 mile) detour to the pier on **Lough Corrib** ❷. Here you can gauge the scale of the lough, which covers 17,000ha (42,000 acres) and is over 43km (26 miles) long. This is one of its widest points, at 22.5km (14 miles); Cong in County Mayo is on the opposite shore. Today, the lough mainly attracts anglers, but in the past it was an important conduit for turf, lime, grain and seaweed to and from Galway docks.

Windswept bog

Cruise of the lough

Corrib Cruises (www.corribcruises. com; phone in advance to confirm) offer daily short tours of the lough from the pier as well as a day trip to **Inchagoill Island**, a romantic spot which has interesting remains of two churches dating from the twelfth and thirteenth centuries, in summer. The cruise continues to Cong, then returns directly to Oughterard.

On the western side of Oughterard is a pretty wooded stretch with a **river walk** beside the Owenriff. Enjoy the trees; they are the last you will see for many miles.

Into Connemara

About 2km (1.2 miles) west of Oughterard the real wilderness scenery begins: low-lying plains, scattered blue lakes and a line of distant

mountains under an enormous sky usually hung with large clouds. The plains are mostly bog-land and in summer you will see heaps of hand-cut turf drying at the side of the road.

After another 14km (8.5 miles), **Maam Cross ❸** is more of a crossroads than a village; the junction with the road to Leenane and the northern shores of Lough Corrib, it was an important place for trading cattle in the old days. A large agricultural fair is still held here every year in August.

Clifden

The road continues for 14km (8.5 miles) to **Recess ❹**, another tiny hamlet, with views in the distant north of the Twelve Bens mountain range. After another 20km (12.5 miles), the road approaches **Clifden ❺**, Connemara's main (arguably only)

Clifden

town. It is pleasantly sited, with two church spires under a wooded peak and above a sea inlet. A compact, lively place, lined with bars, cafés, bookshops and arts-and-crafts galleries, it attracts a wide range of visitors, from artists and hill climbers to Connemara pony enthusiasts. It also has a flourishing lobster fishery and a reputation for good food and comfortable lodgings. Such is its popularity that it has a one-way traffic system; go with the flow around two sides of a triangle, then park. Retrace your steps on foot to browse the shops and galleries. Look out for **Mitchell's Seafood Restaurant**, at the highest point of the triangle, see ❶.

A possible detour just south of Clifden on the R341 Ballyconneely road is a memorial commemorating the landing of the first non-stop transatlantic flight. On 15 June 1919 Alcock and Brown landed their wood and fabric-covered bi-plane nose-first into soft bog after flying for 16 hours and 12 minutes from St John's in Newfoundland, Canada.

Sky Road
At the western end of Market Street the road forks at the Bank of Ireland. Take the right-hand fork uphill, past the Abbeyglen Hotel, for the **Sky Road**. After about 400 metres/yds, look back to see Clifden, with its twin spires and the backdrop of the Twelve Bens. The road continues to rise to about 150 metres (500ft), with views of the beach

below the town and an exhilarating panorama of the islands off Clifden Bay and the open sea beyond. People often say it feels like being on the top of the world. You can opt to drive the 11km (6.5-mile) circuit on narrow, twisting roads, and re-join the N59 northwest of Clifden; this will add about half an hour to your journey.

Northern Connemara
Beyond Clifden, the N59 skirts for 15km (9 miles) around Connemara's western edge and turns east for **Letterfrack** ❻. The village has a few shops and bars, but the best place for some old Irish pub charm is at **Veldons Seafarer Bar & Restaurant**, see ❷. From here, it's a short trip to **Connemara National Park Visitor Centre** (www.connemaranationalpark.ie, free). The park itself, open year-round, is not enclosed, but covers some 2,000ha (4,942 acres) of scenic wilderness. Trails have been marked out of varying degrees of difficulty. The Visitor Centre is a model of its kind, with displays on Connemara's history, fauna, flora and geology, a children's playground, a tearoom and an indoor picnic area.

Kylemore Abbey
Nearby, **Kylemore Abbey** ❼ (www.kylemoreabbey.com, charge), a massive limestone and granite neo-Gothic mansion with battlements above its numerous windows, rears up against a wooded backdrop on the far

A hardy Connemara pony

Food and Drink

① Mitchell's Seafood Restaurant
Market Street, Clifden; www.mitchells restaurantclifden.com
Stone walls, wooden floors and an open fire make an atmospheric restaurant of this former shop. Local mussels are steamed in garlic, while fresh crab is served on home-made bread. Meat eaters and vegetarians both have ample choice. Open March to October only. €€

② Veldons Seafarer Bar & Restaurant
Letterfrack; www.veldons.ie

This atmospheric bar oozes Irish olde world charm with wood panelling and beams, cosy nooks and stove. There's outdoor seating and both the bar and restaurant menus heavily feature fish, as well as the usual pasta, steak and chicken choices. €

③ Hamilton's Bar
Leenane; 095-42266
This old-style pub has a grocery shop in the front, a pool table in the back and a pair of petrol pumps outside, as well as picnic tables. It serves home-made soup and fresh seafood (including open crab or salmon sandwiches). €

side of a reedy lake. It was built in the 1860s by a wealthy local MP for his wife, who died tragically soon after and is commemorated by a tiny Gothic church. Since the 1920s, the building has been home to Benedictine nuns, who ran a prestigious girls' boarding school until 2010. The nuns have restored a large walled Victorian garden, accessible by mini-bus or forest walk. There's also a lovely lakeside walk.

Leenane and Killary Harbour
Leenane ❽ (Leenaun on Sat Nav) is at the inland end of **Killary Harbour**, Ireland's only fjord. On its southern shore, **Killary Fjord Boat Tours** (www.killaryfjord.com, charge) offers 90-minute harbour trips.

In the village – which played a main role in Jim Sheridan's 1990 film *The Field*, based on a John B Keane play – turn left over the bridge to enjoy the long view down the harbour (so long that the sea at its mouth is obscured by mountains), and visit the **Sheep and Wool Centre** (www.sheepand woolcentre.com; mid-Mar–Oct only, free). Here, the O'Toole family demonstrate traditional techniques of spinning, carding, dyeing and weaving wool, the main industry in Leenane a hundred years ago. Some fascinating photos show the village in those days and sheepdog demonstrations can be enjoyed as part of the museum visit. Walk back over the bridge to sample a real Irish pub, **Hamilton's Bar**, see ③.

Kylemore Abbey

TOUR 14
Westport and Mayo

Explore the charms of Westport town, then explore County Mayo with a drive along island-studded Clew Bay to visit Croagh Patrick, Saint Patrick's Holy Mountain. Head inland to the National Museum of Country Life and Foxford Woollen Mills, returning via beautiful Lough Cullin.

DISTANCE: Circular tour: 82km (51 miles)
TIME: 1-hour walk; a half-day drive
START/END: Westport
POINTS TO NOTE: Ballina is 16km (10 miles) north of Foxford, and it is 61km (38 miles) from Ballina to Sligo (tour 15).

Mayo is a large county consisting mainly of bog and mountains, with a coastline battered by the Atlantic. It has long been synonymous with remoteness and poverty, but its unspoilt scenery has made it a popular destination for outdoor lovers.

Westport

Westport ❶ is a compact town of considerable charm, where old Irish ways still prevail. Drive into the centre and park near the highest point. (There is a large car park at the top of Mill Street behind Navin Funeral Home).

The Octagon and Mall
The town was designed in the late eighteenth century by John Browne, the Viscount Westport, to complement his new home, Westport House – making Westport one of just a few planned towns in Ireland. All roads lead to the **Octagon**, the town's marketplace. Around its eight sides are some cut-stone Georgian buildings and at its centre is a statue of Saint Patrick on a tall stone plinth.

Walk down James Street and cross the bridge to take a right on **North Mall**, a tree-lined thoroughfare that runs beside the canalised Carrowbeg River. Turn right at the next bridge up Bridge Street, which has a landmark **clock tower** at its top, as well as the **Tourist Information Office** (www.westporttourism.com). The town has a quirky mix of modern businesses and old traditional ones. Among the latter is a butcher's shop with an art gallery upstairs and a café, **McCormack's Café at the Andrew Stone Gallery**, see ❶.

Westport townhouses

Clew Bay and Westport House

Drive from the Octagon down Quay Hill to the **harbour**. The quays face a beautiful stretch of calm water and the island-studded **Clew Bay**. Many of the old warehouses are now hotels and holiday apartments.

From the quays, turn right facing the water and follow the signs for about 200 metres/yds to reach **Westport House and Pirate Adventure Park** (www.westporthouse.ie; charge, open Mar–Oct). The fine eighteenth-century house in the classical style has period furniture and paintings, but children prefer the funfair and adventure park, with Ireland's only plunge log flume ride and swan-shaped pedalos on the lake. There is also a camping and caravan park.

Croagh Patrick

The R335 to **Murrisk** ❷, 5km (3 miles) west of Westport, is signposted from the quays. It is a scattered, sea-facing fishing village with two pubs; try **The Tavern Bar**, see ❷.

Beyond Murrisk is the car park for pilgrims who intend to climb the Holy Mountain, **Croagh Patrick** ❸, known locally as 'The Reek'.

The cone-shaped peak is almost 800 metres (2,600ft) high and has a small oratory. This is where Saint Patrick is said to have rung his bell to summon Ireland's venomous creatures and cast them from the island. On the last Sunday in July about 30,000 pilgrims make the ascent, some of them barefoot. It takes a fit person about three hours there and back and is well worth the effort for the views of Clew Bay.

Cross the road at the base of Croagh Patrick. Walk beyond a bronze sculpture, the centrepiece of the **Famine Memorial Park**; near the shoreline you will find **Murrisk Abbey**, a traditional starting point for the ascent of the Reek. The ruin of an Augustinian friary, founded in 1456, has some fine stonework in its eastern window.

National Famine Memorial, Murrisk

North of Westport

Return to Westport and take the N5 east through Castlebar for 24km (16 miles) to Turlough.

National Museum of Country Life

The **National Museum of Country Life 4** (www.museum.ie/Country-Life, free) in Turlough Park houses the National Folklife Collection, illustrating traditional ways of life in rural Ireland from 1850 to about 1950. The displays are hugely appealing to both young and old. The award-winning modern building is in the grounds of a former stately home, and there is a good shop and café here.

Foxford Woollen Mills

Follow the N5 east for about 5km (3 miles) and turn north at Bellavary for another 12km (7 miles) to **Foxford 5**. Drive through the village to find the **Foxford Woollen Mills Visitor Centre** (www.foxfordwoollenmills.com). The mill was founded in 1892 to relieve poverty by a remarkable nun; Foxford is known for high-quality tweeds, rugs and blankets. Afterwards, you could make a stop at **The Old Salt Cafe**, see 3, for some provisions to take on the road towards the bleak but rather beautiful loughs around Pontoon.

Pontoon

Cross the bridge over the River Moy and take the R318 west for 7km (4.25 miles) to **Pontoon 6**. Stop at the car park for a great view of Lough Cullin. Pontoon is not a village as such, but a landbridge dividing Lough Cullin from Lough Conn in the north. Turn left on to the R310 to cross it, enjoying views of water on either side. Return to Castlebar on R310, a tour with thriving birdlife (such as snipe and woodcock), and take the N5 west back to Westport.

Food and Drink

1 McCormack's Café at the Andrew Stone Gallery
Bridge Street, Westport; 098-25619
Cakes, quiches and pâtés are displayed in a cold counter, and there are hot specials like bacon and cabbage, or lamb casserole. €

2 The Tavern Bar
Murrisk, www.tavernmurrisk.com
Local fishermen used to arrive here with buckets of langoustines. The menu also includes a selection of cheeses and meat. €

3 The Old Salt Cafe
Main Street, Irishtown, Foxford; 083-091 1189
This cute café is the perfect pitstop for a refuel on-the-go. Pick up gourmet coffee, granola, French toast, waffles and smoothies for breakfast, and burgers, wraps, salads and sandwiches for lunch, or later. Closed Mondays. €

Mayo sheep

Westport, Clew Bay and Croagh Patrick

TOUR 15
Sligo and Donegal

The counties of Sligo and Donegal are stunningly beautiful. County Sligo has a famous literary heritage, awe-inspiring scenery and fabulous beaches, while County Donegal has a quiet, but breathtaking, magnificence.

DISTANCE: 100km (62 miles)
TIME: 1 or 2 days
START: Sligo town
END: Donegal town
POINTS TO NOTE: If you are staying in Sligo town, you could return there after visiting Mullaghmore, rather than continuing on to Donegal town. If you are planning to climb Knocknarea, consider an overnight stay. The best way to Belfast from Donegal is via Omagh and Lisburn. Alternatively, drive via Derry/Londonderry to visit the Giant's Causeway en route.

County Sligo's dramatically carved coastal scenery is a formidable reminder of the last ice age. This tour takes in some of the county's scenic highlights, including Knocknarea mountain and Lough Gill, as well as the literary highlights of Yeats country, before winding north along the coast towards windswept Mullaghmore, the beaches of County Donegal and bustling Donegal town. Linked to the Republic by a slender isthmus, much of Donegal harks back to a remote, rural age. For some here, Irish Gaelic is their first language and, as you head further west into the Gaeltacht area, road signs are written first in Irish and second in English.

Sligo town

Pretty **Sligo town** ❶ is set on the banks of the fast-flowing Garavogue River. Thanks to an enormous rejuvenation project, the town centre is buzzing with shops, cafés and trendy hotels. Sligo hosts an annual W.B. Yeats Summer School (www.yeatssociety.com, charge), which celebrates its most famous literary son. You can visit a Yeats exhibition at the **Sligo County Museum** (Stephen Street; www.sligoarts.ie, free). You will find art by George Russell, Sean Keating and Yeats's brother Jack B. Yeats here, as well as material related to the Irish rebel and suffragette Countess Markievicz (Constance Georgine Gore-Booth, the first woman ever elected to the British parliament). Another cultural highlight is **the Model, home to the Niland Collection** (The

Rosses Point

Mall; www.themodel.ie, free), with exhibitions of contemporary Irish and international art, music performances, cinema events and a strong education programme. **Lyons Café**, see ❶, is a good option for breakfast.

Coastal drive

Leaving Sligo town west on the R292,

you will arrive, after 5km (3 miles), at the beach resort of **Strandhill** ❷. In the daytime, the town attracts families and surfers, thanks to its glorious beach and crashing waves.

For a uniquely relaxing experience, make a visit to the **Voya Seaweed Baths** (seafront; www.voya seaweedbaths.com, charge), where you can submerge yourself in a hot bath of seaweed (known for its skin-smoothing properties) or indulge in a hot-stone massage.

Knocknarea and Carrowmore

Signposted off the coast road (R292), southeast of Strandhill, is the starting-point for ascending **Knocknarea** ❸, 328 metres (1,078ft) above sea level. Perched on top of the mountain is an enormous Neolithic tomb (70 by 11 metres/200 by 35ft), which is said to be the burial place of Queen Mebd (anglicised as 'Maeve'), the warrior queen of Connacht in Celtic mythology. The ascent is steep but worthwhile; the magnificent views

Sligo on the Garavogue

Carrowmore Megalithic Cemetery

Yeats Country

Although the poet and playwright William Butler Yeats (1865–1939) was actually born in Dublin, his family moved to County Sligo soon after his birth. Yeats would come to regard the county as his ancestral and spiritual home. In 'The Lake Isle of Innisfree' Yeats drew inspiration from a small island on Lough Gill, envisaging a place where he might 'live alone in the bee-loud glade'. In one of his last poems, 'Under Ben Bulben', Yeats included a list of instructions for his burial. He was to be buried in Drumcliff churchyard, nestling under 'bare Ben Bulben's head' (referring to the mountain that dominates the Sligo coastline), and the following epitaph was to be written on his gravestone: *'Cast a cold eye/ On life, on death/ Horseman pass by!'* Yeats's requests were carried out to the letter.

Yeats' brother Jack B. Yeats (1871–1951) also derived inspiration from the area. Some of his most memorable paintings are set in and around the county.

suggest why the Celts associated this part of Ireland with myth and magic.

A little further on, just off the R292, is **Carrowmore Megalithic Cemetery** ❹ (www.heritageireland. ie, charge). Ireland's largest megalithic cemetery, it contains 6000-year-old tombs scattered across the hillsides.

Yeats country

Return to the R292 and continue until it meets the R287 to reach tranquil **Lough Gill** ❺, immortalised by W.B. Yeats in the poem 'The Lake Isle of Innisfree'. Rather than driving around the Lough (a detour of some 48km/30 miles), you can stop at a viewing point, signposted just off the R287, by the southwest corner. Return to Sligo via the R287 and R284.

Rosses Point

If you have time, you could make a detour along the R291 (follow the signs, taking a left just past Sligo Harbour) to **Rosses Point**, with its kilometres of beautiful beach, windswept hillside walks and astonishing views both out towards the Atlantic and south towards Knocknarea. The Yeats brothers often spent long, idyllic family holidays at this pleasant spot, wistfully recounted in Yeats's writings.

Drumcliff

About 8km (5 miles) north of Sligo town, on the N15, is the churchyard of **Drumcliff** ❻, Yeats's final resting place. Having died in France in 1939, Yeats was interred here after the Second World War. The spot is delightfully peaceful and Yeats's grave surprisingly unassuming.

Mullaghmore to Rossnowlagh

Signposted off the N15, 12km

Lough Gill from Knocknarea

Slieve League

If you have an extra day to spend in Donegal, the astonishingly beautiful cliffs of Slieve League (a transliteration of the Irish Gaelic, Sliabh Liag, meaning 'grey mountain') are a must. They are among the highest marine cliffs in Europe, 650 metres (2,132ft) above sea level at their most easterly point (nearly three times higher than the more famous Cliffs of Moher). The cliffs are signposted from the R263 at Carrick (An Charraig). You can drive most of the way to the summit; the walk to the highest point takes in craggy towers, stunning mountain-top pools and hardy sheep. The views out towards the Atlantic, and down onto the cliffs below, are breathtaking. Another highlight is the sandy beach resort of Naran on the northern side of the peninsula (off the R261).

Food and Drink

① Lyons Café

Quay Street, Sligo town; www.lyonscafe.com
This Sligo institution is famous for its range of home-baked goodies, especially its scones and chutneys. The lunch specials, such as lamb and pine-nut burgers with feta cheese, offer a contemporary twist. €

a small stretch of County Leitrim).

The first resort along the N15 is **Bundoran**. Bundoran actually marks the point at which County Donegal's 13 Blue Flag beaches begin. Between here and Donegal town, any turn off the main road will take you to one of these beaches; **Rossnowlagh** is recommended.

Donegal town

Some 30km (18.5 miles) from Bundoran, following the N15 north, is lively **Donegal town ❽**, with its busy triangular 'Diamond' market square. It is a place of contrasts, as Irish-speaking locals encounter tourists in a town that contains as many high-street chains as it does craft shops and tearooms. Set on the River Eske, it is notable for its riverside **castle**, built by the O'Donnell family in the fifteenth century and redesigned by the Brookes, planters who took over the town in the seventeenth century.

(7.5 miles) north of Drumcliff, is the coast road to **Mullaghmore ❼**, with its vast swathe of golden sand and picture-postcard harbour. Before leaving Mullaghmore, follow the coastal road round to take in windswept **Mullaghmore Head**.

County Donegal beaches

Leave Mullaghmore by the road that sweeps northeast along the coast to return to the N15. After 8km (5 miles) you will pass into County Donegal (via

Mullaghmore   Yeats's grave

WALK 16
Belfast

Belfast is full of impressive Victorian architecture, chic bars and restaurants. Wander around its quirky museums, grand gardens and fabulous library that collide in a city that buzzes with energy.

DISTANCE: 2.5 miles (4km)
TIME: A full day
START: Botanic Gardens
END: CastleCourt Centre
TO NOTE: Buses (no. 8) run from Queen's Quarter, north to Donegall Square. Buses (Metro 26 takes 20 minutes) to the Titanic Quarter depart from Wellington Place, on the northwest corner of Donegall Square, and also stop at the Albert Clock Tower. Walkers can follow the Titanic Trail signposts from the City Hall – allow 40 minutes. If you plan to take a black-taxi tour of west Belfast, it is advisable to book in the morning before you set out. Arrange for the drivers to pick you up somewhere central like Donegall Square. Belfast is very quiet on Sundays, when shops and city-centre restaurants tend to be open 1–6pm. Dublin is about 170km (105 miles) south of Belfast via the A1 and M1. Regular trains connect Belfast Central and Dublin's Connolly Station, taking 2–2.25 hours.

Belfast's dominant Victorian and Edwardian architecture resembles more a northern English city, such as Leeds or Liverpool, than the softer Georgian elegance of Dublin. But Northern Ireland's capital has other attributes. A low-rise, open city, framed between lofty green Cave Hill and the great blue bowl of Belfast Lough, it is dotted with lovely parks and open spaces and, for a major city, is surprisingly easy to get around. Above all, it's the people of Belfast who remain its great attraction. Despite preconceptions, they are among the friendliest you will meet, with an easy and down-to-earth sense of humour.

Belfast was the birthplace of the legendary *Titanic*, the most luxurious of liners built in the port's Edwardian heyday. Pride in this legacy is exemplified by the £97m visitor centre, **Titanic Belfast** in the former dockyards. The city offers a centre rich in historical and artistic legacy, with a vibrant bar and restaurant scene. A century after its golden age, Belfast has come back into its own.

Queen's University

Queen's Quarter

Based around Victorian architect Sir Charles Lanyon's distinguished Queen's University, Queen's Quarter is an eclectic mix of elegant wine-bars, scruffy student diners, quirky bookshops and plenty of impressive architecture.

Botanic Gardens

Begin the walk at the tranquil **Botanic Gardens ❶** (between College Park and Stranmillis Road, free), laid out in the mid-nineteenth century. Make sure to visit Sir Charles Lanyon's restored curvilinear **Palm House**, and the **Tropical Ravine**, both of which contain exotic flora. Also within the garden is the superb **Ulster Museum** (www. nmni.com/um, free), where the wonderful collection ranges from natural history to contemporary art.

Palm House in the Botanic Gardens

Queen's University

Leave the gardens by the Stranmillis Road exit and walk north along University Road. On the right is the imposing courtyard and red-brick facade of **Queen's University ❷**, which Lanyon based on Magdalen College, Oxford. There are more than one hundred listed buildings around the campus and surrounding area; to learn more you can visit the **Welcome Centre** (www.qub.ac.uk/home/welcome-centre, free), which also organises guided tours.

Botanic Avenue

Leave University Road by University Square, lined with Victorian terraces, to arrive at College Park, which leads to student-filled **Botanic Avenue**. Look out for vibrant and ever-popular **French Village Café and Bistro** (at no. 99), a great stop for morning-after coffee, breakfast and smoothies see ❶. The excellent crime bookshop **No Alibis** (at no. 83; www.noalibis.com) is well worth exploring too.

South of the city centre

Shaftesbury Square, at the top of Botanic Avenue, was once an integral part of Belfast's 'Golden Mile', established during the Troubles to boost the city's tourism. However, the Golden Mile has suffered from a lack of regeneration and a decline in popularity.

Ulster Hall

Leading off from the top right-hand corner of Shaftesbury Square, the Dublin Road becomes Bedford Street, home of the distinguished **Ulster Hall** (no. 34; www.ulsterhall.co.uk), a historical gem dating from 1862. It opened as a music hall, and now hosts sporting events, rock gigs, classical music concerts, and is currently home to the Ulster Orchestra. An informative display tells its history.

Great Victoria Street

Turn left beyond the Ulster Hall for Great Victoria Street. On the corner is the glorious **Crown Liquor Saloon ❸** (no. 46; www.nicholsonspubs.co.uk/thecrown liquorsaloonbelfast). One of the world's most beautiful Victorian pubs, it was elegantly restored by the National Trust on the advice of the poet John Betjeman. Its ten wood-panelled snugs, which were once used by prostitutes, are now fought over by a more salubrious clientele.

Across the road is the 4-star **Europa Hotel**, which achieved the dubious fame of being 'the most bombed hotel in Europe' during the Troubles. Continue north to another ornate building. **The Grand Opera House** (tours Thu and Sat 11am), topped by white minarets, dates from 1895. Cross the road and turn right (east) into Wellington Place for Donegall Square.

Ulster Hall

Donegall Square

Donegall Square, dominated by the City Hall, is the heart of the city centre. **Belfast Welcome Centre** (47 Donegall Place; www.visitbelfast.com, free), to the north of the square, is packed full of useful information.

Linen Hall Library

On the northwestern corner of Donegall Square is the quirky **Linen Hall Library ❹** (no. 17; www.linen hall.com, free). Belfast's oldest library, it was founded in 1788 as the Belfast Reading Society and later renamed to reflect the city's linen-producing heritage. Nowadays, it contains an intriguing selection of books and newspapers, comfortable armchairs and a small café.

City Hall

The massive **City Hall ❺** (www.belfastcity.gov.uk, free), also known as 'the stone Titanic' (the same craftsmen worked on both projects), dominates the square.

Fully renovated, this huge Renaissance Revival-style Edwardian gem, built in 1906, was inspired by London's St Paul's, and has an ornate cathedral-like interior. Even if you don't take a tour, nip in for an eyeful. The **Titanic Memorial Garden** is a favourite lunchtime spot in summer and the many monuments here include Thomas Brock's statue of Queen Victoria, and his Titanic Memorial.

WALK 16   WATERFRONT

Black cab taxi tours

An excellent way of seeing west Belfast – particularly the graphic murals of the (Catholic) Falls and (Protestant) Shankill roads and the peace line built to keep the two areas apart – is by a black-cab tour. Some cab companies are better than others and not all go to the less sanitised Shankill area, where the murals are fresher, and angrier. The tours give an invaluable insight into the political and social reality of the Troubles. A good company is Paddy Campbell's Belfast Black Cab Tours (www.belfastblackcabtours. co.uk). A one-hour 30-minute tour costs around £35 for 1–2 people (or £12 each for 3–6 people).

Waterfront

Leave Donegall Square in the direction of the waterfront along May Street. After some 250 metres/ yds you will find the neoclassical **Royal Courts of Justice** (1933). Facing them, on the right-hand side of the street, is **St George's Market ❻** (www.stgeorgesmarket.com). Built in 1896 for the sale of fruit, butter, eggs and poultry, it is one of the best markets in operation in Ireland. Hugely popular and held on Fridays, Saturdays and Sundays, stalls sell a host of fresh food and other goods including antiques,

City Hall

Linen Hall Library interior

Giant's Causeway

If you have a day to spare, the Giant's Causeway, a 2-hour drive north of Belfast (taking the A26), is highly recommended. The existence of the Causeway – an astonishing assembly of more than 40,000 basalt columns, formed into packed hexagonal shapes by the cooling of molten lava – was not even known about until the Bishop of Derry stumbled upon it in 1692. Although the columns are relatively small – the tallest is only about 12 metres (39ft) high – the sight of them extending further out to sea, in the shadow of craggy red mountains, is breathtaking. Entrance is via the Giant's Causeway Visitor Experience (Causeway Head; www.nationaltrust.org.uk/giants-causeway, charge), 2 miles (3km) north of Bushmills on the B146.

crafts and books. The **market stalls** offer an excellent choice for an impromptu lunch or snack, see ②.

Laganside

Waterfront Hall
After leaving the market, turn left onto Oxford Street and right onto the pedestrianised area by the **Belfast Waterfront Hall** (2 Lanyon Place; www.waterfront.co.uk, free). The

glass-fronted galleries, which visitors are open to explore, afford views over Belfast and the River Lagan.

Continuing north along the riverside, pass under Sir Charles Lanyon's 1843 **Queen's Bridge**, and the modern Queen Elizabeth Bridge, to Lagan Weir. The colourful **Big Fish** sculpture has tiles depicting aspects of Belfast's history. This is the embarkation point for the *Titanic* Boat Tour (www.laganboatcompany.com, charge).

At the northern end of Donegall Quay is the elegant mid-nineteenth century **Custom House**, another of Lanyon's fabulous architectural achievements.

Titanic Quarter

To walk to the **Titanic Quarter** ❼ follow the signposts across the river. The Odyssey (www.theodyssey.co.uk) is a huge indoor arena used for basketball and rock concerts, which also houses the extremely enjoyable W5 (www.w5online.co.uk, charge), a science and discovery centre for children.

Titanic Belfast (www.titanicbelfast.com, charge, last admission 1hr 40mins before closing) is an unmissable landmark, an architectural extravaganza clad in anodized aluminium, echoing the height and proportions of the gigantic ship's prow. Nine galleries on six storeys give you the tragic story

Titanic's Dock and Pump House

Food and Drink

① French Village Botanic

99 Botanic Avenue,
www.frenchvillagebelfast.co.uk/
botanic

Popular with students from Queen's, alternatively recovering and reloading, this place is always buzzing. Their eclectic offering ranges from brilliant breakfasts through to an excellent à la carte evening menu (try the Bang Bang chicken with Asian vegetables and triple-cooked chips), via various good-all-day pastries and drinks. Veggie options are good, and the set menu (for six) is excellent value. BYOB available, £3 corkage. ££

② St George's Market

12–20 East Bridge Street

This brilliant market offers an amazing variety of lunch options. Choose from crêpes, fresh pasta, hog-roast sandwiches, home-made cakes or Chinese, Indian and Mexican food, and eat it in the central-seating area while listening to a live band. £

③ Muriel's

12–14 Church Lane, www.facebook.com/muriels.cafebar

This tiny café morphs into a cocktail bar in the evening and has firmly established its reputation among Belfast's hipsters. The brunches and lunches – eggs Benedict, Mexican-style sandwiches and seafood platters – are particularly popular. ££

of the ship from her conception to her sinking on 14 April 1912, and its aftermath. Another site nearby associated with the Titanic is the compelling **Titanic's Dock and Pump House** (www.titanics dock.com, charge), where the ship stood while being fitted out.

Shoppers' Belfast

Leaving the riverside area at the Custom House and heading down High Street brings you to the **Albert Memorial Clock Tower**, constructed by Queen Victoria in her husband's memory between

1865 and 1870. It leans 1.25 metres (4ft) off the vertical, rendering it Belfast's very own 'leaning tower'. About 50 metres/yds past the Clock Tower, a left turn down Church Lane, home of the excellent café-bar **Muriel's**, see ③, will take you to a shopper's paradise.

The sprawling shopping destination, **Victoria Square ⑧** (www.victoriasquare.com) has shops over four levels. The shopping streets of Ann Street, Cornmarket and Castle Street lead to Royal Avenue, home of the older, larger **CastleCourt Centre ⑨** (www.castlecourt-uk.com).

Giant's Causeway   Titanic Belfast

DIRECTORY

Our edit of the best hotels, restaurants and evening entertainment to suit all tastes and budgets, plus an A–Z of all the essential information you need to know, and some great book and film recommendations to give you a flavour of the country.

Accommodation

At the top end of Ireland's hotel offering are the grand city landmarks, elegant castles and country houses. The middle range includes new hotels with elaborate spa facilities and lovingly converted period buildings. The inexpensive hotels tend to be family-owned or guesthouses (just like a hotel, but with no bar or restaurant). Most B&Bs come into the economy category, but even so, you can expect an en-suite bathroom and a good standard of comfort (plus a hearty Irish breakfast, of course).

Book in advance June–Sept and for Dublin year-round. If you are staying for more than one night, ask for a reduced rate. Book either directly with the hotel or through www.discoverireland.com, which also lists self-catering options.

Both the Irish Republic and Northern Ireland classify hotels on broadly the same grading system, as follows:
***** Top-grade hotels, some in former castles; all rooms have private bathrooms and suites are available. High-quality restaurant.
**** Hotels, ranging from modern, purpose-built premises to converted period houses, offering a high standard of comfort and service. With a few exceptions, all rooms have private bathrooms.
*** Medium-priced hotels, ranging from small, family-run places to larger,

Price categories

Price for a double room for one night with breakfast in the Republic of Ireland:
€€€€ = over 300 euros
€€€ = over 200 euros
€€ = under 200 euros
€ = under 100 euros
Price for a double room for one night with breakfast in Northern Ireland:
££££ = over £200
£££ = £150–200
££ = £80–150
£ = under £80

more commercial operations. Most of the rooms have private bathrooms.
** Mostly family-run hotels, with a limited but satisfactory range of food and comfort. Some rooms have private bathrooms.
* Simple but acceptable accommodation and services.

Dublin

Aberdeen Lodge
53–55 Park Avenue; www.aberdeen-lodge.com
A large three-storey Victorian house in the elegant south Dublin area of Ballsbridge, with really spacious bedrooms, all beautifully furnished. Regular buses run to the city centre, and it is also close to Sydney Parade DART station. €€€

The Clarence, Dublin

Ariel House
50 Lansdowne Road; www.ariel-house.net
Elegant Victorian-style redbrick
guesthouse in leafy inner suburb, with
a modern wing of large comfortable
bedrooms. Renowned for its breakfast
and the friendly welcome. €€

Buswell's Hotel
23–7 Molesworth Street; www.buswells.ie/en
Georgian town houses used as a hotel
since the 1920s, oozing period charm.
A haunt of politicians because of its
proximity to Leinster House. €€€

The Charles Stewart
5–6 Parnell Square; 01 878 0350
This lovely guesthouse in a Georgian
property is right on Parnell Square
(named, of course, for Charles
Stewart Parnell), near a bus stop
to the airport. The rooms are well
maintained; the young staff is helpful
and enthusiastic. Excellent value. €€

The Clarence
6–8 Wellington Quay; www.theclarence.ie
Central, riverside location, backing
onto Temple Bar. Refurbished and
redesigned, but still retaining its
keynote Art Deco panelling with stylish
restraint, this place delights the eye
as well as the stomach (the restaurant
is first class). Former owners include
members of the U2 rock group and the
clientele is self-consciously hip. €€€€

Clayton Hotel Ballsbridge
Merrion Road; www.claytonhotelballsbridge.com
A large, excellent-value hotel next
to the RDS Arena, in a converted
Victorian Masonic School. Over
300 rooms are offered at a flat per-
room rate, with tea/coffee-making
facilities. There is also a lively lounge
bar and a good restaurant. €€

Harcourt Hotel
60 Harcourt Street; www.harcourthotel.ie
Harcourt occupies a row of Georgian
houses just off St Stephen's Green.
Rooms are small, and can be noisy as the
hotel has a nightclub, but the location
and ambience make it good value. €€

The Hoxton - Central Hotel
2 Exchequer Street; https://thehoxton.ie-dublin.eu
Close to both Grafton Street and
Temple Bar, this rambling Victorian
hotel has an excellent location, and
a mildly Bohemian atmosphere.
Its cosy first-floor Library Bar is
a haunt of literary types. €€€

The Merrion Hotel
Upper Merrion Street; www.merrionhotel.com
A luxurious 5-star hotel, converted
from four Georgian town houses, with
a pool, spa and gym. Individually
designed rooms and suites, each with
beautiful bathrooms. So discreet it even
lacks a hotel sign, using instead a small,
traditional Georgian brass plaque. €€€€

Number 31
31 Lesson Close; www.number31.ie
Combining a classic Georgian town
house with a Modernist 1960s mews

designed by noted architect Sam Stephenson, this beautiful hotel is situated close to Fitzwilliam Square. Famous for its excellent breakfasts and unique 'sunken lounge'. €€€€

O'Callaghan Davenport
Merrion Square; www.ocallaghanhotels.com
This elegant 4-star hotel is well situated for the city centre, Merrion Square and Trinity College. Rooms are large, comfortable and surprisingly good value. €€€€

Hotel St George
7 Parnell Square; www.hotelstgeorgedublin.com
This cosy Georgian town house has a real 'old Dublin' feel and the central location, off O'Connell St, offers unbeatable value. The interior rooms overlooking the garden are quieter. €

The Westbury Hotel
Grafton Street; www.doylecollection.com
Consistently rated one of the most popular hotels in Dublin, the Westbury Hotel is a Dublin institution due to its 5-star luxury, city centre location, excellent restaurant and its afternoon tea. €€€€

The Wilder
22 St Stephens Green; www.thewilder.ie
Luxury boutique hotel with gin and tearooms serving an award-winning breakfast in a wonderful central location in Georgian Dublin; handy for shopping. €€€

Around Dublin: County Wicklow
Ashton House
Meetings of the Water, Vale of Avoca; 0402-35535
A lovely guesthouse with beautiful gardens, located right at the Meeting of the Waters. Next door to the Meetings pub for traditional Irish music sessions and a perfect pint of Guinness. €

Woodenbridge Hotel & Lodge
Vale of Avoca, Arklow (on the R752); www.woodenbridgehotel.com
Established in 1608, this hotel is one of the oldest in Ireland. A bargain for County Wicklow, with bright, spacious rooms, a decent breakfast and lovely views over the Vale of Avoca. Choose the more modern Lodge to be away from the busier main hotel. €

Southeast: Kilkenny
Butler House
16 Patrick Street, Kilkenny city; www.butler.ie
Once the Dower House of Kilkenny Castle, the reception rooms here have ornate plaster ceilings and marble fireplaces, while the bedrooms have clean-lined modern decor. Breakfast is served in the Design Centre, a short walk across the garden. There's no bar or restaurant, but you are right in the centre of town. Book well in advance. €€€

Mount Juliet Estate
Thomastown, County Kilkenny; www.mountjuliet.ie
This elegant 18th-century house is the centrepiece of a 600ha (1,500-acre) estate

The Westbury Hotel, Dublin

by the River Nore, which includes a Jack Nicklaus-designed golf course, equestrian centre, fishing, archery, falconry, tennis and luxury spa. Rooms in the main house have impeccable period decor plus modern facilities, albeit at a price. Dine at the Michelin-starred Lady Helen or the less formal Hunter's Yard. €€€€

Zuni Townhouse
26 Patrick Street, Kilkenny city; www.zuni.ie
Town-centre boutique hotel with minimalist decor, free parking, chic cocktail bar and a popular restaurant serving modern Irish food with influences from around the globe. €€€

Southeast: Waterford & Cashel

Bailey's Hotel Cashel
**42 Main Street, Cashel;
www.baileyshotelcashel.com**
A sympathetically restored Georgian building in the centre of Cashel. Free entry into the Rock of Cashel with every booking. Comfortable surroundings with underfloor heating. €€

Dooley's Hotel
The Quay, Waterford city; www.dooleys-hotel.ie
Family-run hotel with good food and lively bar in centre of town, on the River Suir. €€

Granville Hotel
The Quay, Waterford city; www.granvillehotel.ie
Birthplace of Thomas Francis Meagher – a freedom fighter who introduced the tricolour flag to Ireland – the Granville's

porticoed entrance has been a landmark on Waterford's quays for generations. The hotel has retained its Georgian character through many refurbishments, but remains likeably old fashioned. It is perfectly located for exploring the city on foot. €€€

Southwest: Cork city and environs

Ballymaloe House
Shanagarry, Midleton; www.ballymaloe.ie
One of Ireland's finest country house hotels and one of the world's leading cookery schools, Ballymaloe is set in a beautiful part of East Cork. The kitchen is renowned for its pioneering use of fresh local produce, including home-grown vegetables and ripe fruit from the hotel's own farm. It is less than an hour's drive east of Cork city off the N25. €€€€

Clayton Hotel Cork City
Lapp's Quay, Cork; www.claytonhotelcorkcity.com
A large hotel in the centre of town by the River Lee, the Clayton is a pioneer of the ongoing docklands development. There's a central atrium with a wide staircase, which some bedrooms overlook; if you want an exterior view, say so. Bedrooms have chic, minimalist decor, while the bar extends on to a riverside walk and is a popular early evening spot. €€

Gabriel House
Summerhill North, St Luke's Cross, Cork; www.gabriel-house.ie
This large detached building was previously a Christian Brothers seminary,

O'Callaghan Davenport hotel

but now makes a characterful guesthouse from which to explore the city. It's on a bluff high above the railway station, a five-minute walk uphill from the centre; the best and largest rooms have a river view. €€

Hotel Isaacs
48 MacCurtain Street, Cork; www.hotelisaacscork.com

Charming Victorian hotel with contemporary interior tucked away under an archway off a busy road. Handy for both bus and train stations. €

Southwest: West Cork
Old Presbytery
43 Cork Street, Kinsale; www.oldpres.com

Characterful old town house furnished with an attractive medley of antiques and offering a high standard of comfort. There is self-catering accommodation available in an annexe to the main building. Quiet town-centre location. €€€

Rolf's Country House
Baltimore Hill, Baltimore; https://rolfscountryhouse.com

A converted old stone-built farmhouse and outbuildings on a site high above Roaring Water Bay. Bedrooms are small and simple, with white cotton bedlinen and casement windows, and there are self-catering cottages available. The restaurant is pleasantly informal, with exhibitions by local artists. The village is about 1.5km (1 mile) away and has a lively pub and café scene in summer. €€€

Trident Hotel
Kinsale; www.tridenthotel.com

Watch the boats come and go from this modern waterside hotel, adjacent to the town pier, where all rooms have sea views. The Wharf Tavern is popular with locals for bar food. €€€

Southwest: Ring of Kerry
Butler Arms Hotel
Waterville; www.butlerarms.com

Well-established, informal hotel overlooking the sea that has been run by the same family since 1916. Golf, tennis, shooting and fishing. The cast and crew of Star Wars stayed here when filming *The Force Awakens*. €€€

Carrig Country House
Caragh Lake, Glenbeigh; www.carrighouse.com

You can hear the waters of the lake lapping from your bedroom in this magical hideaway. The Victorian manor house is set in carefully tended lakeside gardens, with views of the wild mountains. Bedrooms are furnished in Victorian style with antique furniture; the peaceful sitting room is lined with books; and the restaurant is excellent. €€€€

Loch Lein Country House Hotel
Fossa, Killarney; www.lochlein.com

Situated 4km (2.5 miles) outside Killarney just off the main Ring of Kerry (N72), this 25-room hotel makes an excellent touring base. It occupies a secluded location with tantalising views of Loch Lein across the fields. €€€

Mount Juliet Estate grounds

Parknasilla Resort and Spa
Sneem; www.parknasillaresort.com

Set amid 200ha (500 acres) of balmy sub-tropical vegetation on a sheltered sea inlet, with a dramatic backdrop of mountains, this is one of Ireland's most famous resort hotels. Opt for a room in the main house or the less expensive self-catering lodges (two bedrooms) and villas (three bedrooms). The bedrooms have been fully upgraded, as have the pool and spa, while the lounge and bar retain a mildly eccentric old-fashioned charm. €€€€

Sea Lodge Waterville
Waterville; www.sealodgewaterville.ie

Luxurious, modern boutique hotel with a nautical theme. Stunning views across Ballinskelligs Bay. The village of Waterville was Charlie Chaplin's favourite holiday destination and the village hosts an annual Charlie Chaplin festival. €€€

Southwest: Dingle Peninsula/Tralee

Ballygarry House Hotel and Spa
Killarney Road, Tralee; www.ballygarryhouse.com

This family run country house-style hotel has been extended without losing the quiet charm of the original. Located 2.5km (1.5 miles) outside town, it is a great touring base, with mountain views, and forest walking trails on the doorstep. The bar has a large local clientele, and the restaurant is a favourite for special occasions, while residents can enjoy their own drawing room and library. The spa is excellent. €€€

Dingle Skellig Hotel
Dingle; www.dingleskellig.com

Well-designed modern hotel on the water's edge. Sea view on request. Indoor pool and spa. Renowned for its family-friendly ethos. €€€

Greenmount House
Upper John Street, Dingle; www.greenmounthouse.ie

Although only a short walk from the town centre, this quiet 14-room guesthouse is surrounded by country fields and has a lovely view of the sun setting over Dingle Harbour. Rooms are spacious, with uncluttered contemporary decor. The home-baking and breakfast here are famous. €€€

West: Limerick and Shannon

Dromoland Castle
Newmarket-on-Fergus, County Clare; www.dromoland.ie

If you can only sample one luxury castle hotel, choose this one. Once the ancestral home of the O'Briens, direct descendants of Brian Ború who defeated the Vikings in 1014, the baronial-style hotel has splendid views over the lake and golf course. Even though the public rooms are awe-inspiringly grand, staff are so friendly that guests quickly feel at home. €€€€

Dunraven Arms Hotel
Adare, County Limerick; www.dunravenhotel.com

Beautifully refurbished historic inn in picture-book pretty village. Equestrian and golf holidays are a speciality. €€€

Limerick and the Shannon at dusk

Fitzgerald's Woodlands House Hotel
Knockanes, Adare, County Limerick;
www.woodlands-hotel.ie

This unpretentious, friendly family-run hotel about 1.5km (1 mile) outside Adare is a good touring base, within easy reach of Shannon Airport. It has a lively bistro and a more formal restaurant. Constant additions and refurbishment have also given it a pool, a large gym and an above-average spa. €€

West: the Cliffs of Moher and the Burren

Gregan's Castle
Ballyvaughan, County Clare;
www.gregans.ie

This is one of Ireland's finest country house hotels, a quiet retreat at the base of the Burren's famous Corkscrew Hill, with breathtaking views over Galway Bay. The elegant decor features fine antiques and contemporary Irish art. A warm welcome and a renowned restaurant make it a favourite hideaway. Be warned, there is only one TV in the house. €€€€

Hyland's Burren Hotel
Ballyvaughan, County Clare;
www.hylandsburren.com

Hyland's is a typical, much-extended nineteenth-century village-centre hotel with a restaurant and lively bar. Most rooms have glorious views of the surrounding limestone hills. €€€

West: Galway city

The G
Wellpark; www.theghotel.ie

Dedicated followers of fashion will not mind paying a premium to experience a wildly different hotel with an extravagant sense of fun and great art on the walls. Designed by hat-maker extraordinaire Philip Treacy, the colourful reception rooms contrast with the soothingly tranquil bedrooms. It also has a seriously good spa. €€€€

Glenlo Abbey Hotel
Bushy Park; www.glenloabbeyhotel.ie

Luxuriously converted monastery on the banks of Lough Corrib, 4km (2.5 miles) west of the city centre, surrounded by its own golf course. Other activities include yoga, falconry and fishing. Treat yourself to afternoon tea aboard a 1940s train carriage in the Pullman Restaurant. €€€€

The Hardiman
Eyre Square; www.thehardiman.ie

Grand old railway hotel on the city's main square, formerly the Grand Meyrick; still a major landmark with luxury 4-star accommodation and all the bells and whistles, including afternoon tea, a cocktail bar and brasserie. €€€

The House Hotel
Spanish Parade; www.thehousehotel.ie

A stylish boutique hotel with a prime location in Galway's Latin Quarter, the House makes a memorable – and convenient – base in the centre of

Dromoland Castle, County Clare

the shopping and pubbing district. Bedrooms in this warehouse conversion are compact but comfortable, with snazzy contemporary decor. The real star here is the House Cocktail Bar (with live music at weekends). €€€

Park House Hotel
Forster Street, Eyre Square;
www.parkhousehotel.ie
An old stone warehouse has been converted and extended to create a welcoming hotel. Bedrooms have warm decor and are sufficiently glazed to mute noisy Galway nightlife. Right in the city centre, the bar and lobby area are favourites with locals. €€€

West: Connemara
Abbeyglen Castle Hotel
Sky Road, Clifden, County Galway;
www.abbeyglen.ie
A delightfully old-fashioned manor house hotel, superbly located on a height above Clifden Bay in extensive gardens (but just a short walk from town), this is an ideal base for touring Connemara. The room price includes afternoon tea, a great rainy-day treat. Rooms vary in size and aspect; the best ones are in the front of the house, but all have an old-world charm. At night the bar and restaurant are lively spots. €€

Ardagh Hotel
Ballyconneely Road, Clifden, County Galway; www.ardaghhotel.com
Quiet, family-run hotel 2km (1.2 miles)

from Clifden on Ardbear Bay. Excellent restaurant specialising in seafood. €€€

Ashford Castle
Cong, County Mayo; www.ashfordcastle.com
A fairytale castle, standing between loughs Corrib and Mask, Ashford never fails to impress. American-owned, it has very high standards of comfort and decor, a private golf course, tennis, fishing, boating, horse riding, falconry, shooting and extensive gardens. €€€€

West: Westport town
Knockranny House Hotel
Castlebar Road, Westport;
www.knockrannyhousehotel.ie
Large, luxurious hotel on the edge of town with splendid views of Croagh Patrick, an excellent restaurant and award-winning spa. €€€

Westport Plaza, Westport Coast and Castlecourt Hotel
Castlebar Street, Westport town;
www.westporthotelgroup.ie
These sister-hotels in the centre of Westport are run by the same family, and share a leisure centre and spa, but have separate identities. The less expensive Castlecourt is a comfortable, traditional hotel catering for holiday and business clients, while the more chic (and expensive) Plaza is a boutique-style hotel with Chesterfield sofas in its reception area and pleasantly luxurious bedrooms. The Coast is the only waterfront hotel in Westport, and has stunning views over Clew Bay. €€€

Dunraven Arms Hotel, Adare

Northwest: Sligo town

Sligo Southern Hotel
Strandhill Road; www.sligosouthernhotel.ie

A 'superior' 3-star hotel, right in the centre of town, with its own leisure centre, Orient Express bar with live music on Saturday nights, and garden room restaurant. Although the interior is a little faded, the hotel is excellent value; consider upgrading to a suite for great views and a private Jacuzzi. €€

Sligo Park Hotel
Pearse Road; www.sligoparkhotel.com

Scenic location 1.5km (1 mile) south of town with gardens and leisure centre. Appeals to families with great-value packages. €€

Northwest: Donegal town

Ard na Breatha Guesthouse
Drumrooske Middle; www.ardnabreatha.com

An award-winning guesthouse 2km (1.2 miles) outside Donegal town. The bedrooms are bright and spacious. Breakfast choices include the 'full Irish', smoked salmon and pancakes. Highly recommended. €€

Harvey's Point Country Hotel
Lough Eske; www.harveyspoint.com

Modern luxurious lakeside complex with sports facilities. The award-winning restaurant is a huge draw, as are the well-appointed rooms. €€€

Mill Park
The Mullins; www.millparkhotel.com

A large hotel close to Donegal town, with a choice of rooms and suites, a leisure centre (including pool, sauna and steam room) and a restaurant specialising in seafood. €€

Northern Ireland: Belfast

Benedicts Hotel
7–21 Bradbury Place; www.benedictshotel.co.uk

Good value boutique-style hotel with an excellent restaurant, which uses local produce. ££

House Belfast
59–63 Botanic Avenue; 028-9531 3120

This warm 31-room hotel with inviting rooms near Queen's University boasts a main bar with a cherry blossom tree at its heart, a mezzanine bar area, a function room, a café and a wooden-clad whiskey room. ££

The Merchant Hotel
16 Skipper Street; www.themerchanthotel.com

Located in the arty Cathedral Quarter, this hotel has come to epitomise Belfast's new identity as a hot destination. Housed in what was once the headquarters of Ulster Bank, the huge former banking hall is now the breathtakingly grand Great Room Restaurant. ££££

Tara Lodge
36 Cromwell Road; www.taralodge.com

Well located just off Botanic Avenue, Tara Lodge combines the facilities of a hotel with the friendliness of a guesthouse. The rooms are spacious and comfortable and the staff helpful. ££

Ashford Castle, County Mayo

Destination Hotel | Stay Lagom - Ballycastle

For those in search of a unique destination stay along the Causeway Coastal Route, Stay Lagom (11 Novally Road, Ballycastle, BT546HB, https://stay lagom.com) provides the perfect base. A stone's throw from the North Coast's UNESCO Giants Causeway other top sights such as Dunluce Castle and Carrick-a-Rede rope bridge, it's the perfect hub to venture out from. Situated off a quiet road and set amid the walled gardens of a charming Georgian estate dating back to the 1800's, Lagom is the perfect mix of modern meets traditional. Designed by travellers for travellers, the owners have thought of everything, accommodating families, individuals, couples or groups. The accommodation itself ranges from private ensuite rooms, pet-friendly abodes, futuristic pods, or separate luxurious self-contained lodges. Take a room or if it's the full extended family you can book out the whole place accommodating up to 31 guests. All guests have access

to kitchen facilities, remote working and lounge areas, onsite bike hire, laundry, EV charging and superfast broadband!

To plan your day; sightseeing tours and various experiences can be booked directly online through Lagom too – consider a boat trip out to Rathlin Island, follow a Traditional Music Trail led by local musicians, hit the greens on one of the many Links awarded golf courses or indulge in a sumptuous spa day. After a long day exploring, guests will be more than happy to return to their lovely bolthole at Lagom and fall into the comfiest bed.

With so much to see, do, taste, and hear, we would highly recommend staying on the North Coast for at least three to four nights. Lagom does book out quickly, so if you get lucky enough to stay here, take the opportunity.

Scan the QR code to find out more

Ten Square Hotel
10 Donegal Square South; www.tensquare.co.uk
A listed Victorian linen warehouse has been transformed into an ultra-luxurious hotel with oriental decor and an emphasis on style. Right in the centre of town, on Donegal Square. £££

Youth Hostels

The Irish Youth Hostel Association, An Óige, has a website (www.anoige. ie) with an excellent choice of hostels throughout the Republic. For hostels in Northern Ireland, visit Hostelling International NI (www.hini.org.uk).

Restaurants

After years in the gastronomic wilderness, Ireland has embraced modern cooking with great enthusiasm. Some of the best restaurants in the country are still to be found in hotels, but they are a far cry from the days of overcooked meat and soggy vegetables. Now, a light-handed approach allows the natural flavours of fresh local produce to shine through. Nowhere in Ireland is more than a two-hour drive from the sea, and fresh seafood is a much-prized ingredient. Indeed, these days Cork is known as the foodie capital of the country and its proximity to the sea ensures that local restaurants have access to an abundance of fresh ingredients.

The Irish dining scene is consistently informal: even the grandest hotels specify 'smart but casual', meaning a jacket for men, but no obligatory tie. Advance booking is advisable at weekends and in summer.

While the cities generally have a wide range of small restaurants, in the countryside pubs are more often than not a major element in the eating-out scene. Many are now more like restaurants than the drinking dens of yore, and most welcome children during daylight hours. Outdoor tables are commonplace; the only thing you need is the weather to be able to enjoy them.

Price categories

Price guide for a two-course dinner for one in the Republic of Ireland:
€€€€ = over €50
€€€ = €30–50
€€ = €20–30
€ = under €20
Price guide for a two-course dinner for one in Northern Ireland:
££££ = over £40
£££ = £25–40
££ = £15–25
£ = under £15

Dublin

777
7 Castle House, South Great George's Street; www.777.ie
Fun Mexican restaurant with bold flavours and vibrant colours located in the city centre. They have Dublin's largest selection of tequilas and are as such famous for their Margaritas. Come for latter and the tapas-style menu with reasonably-priced dishes to share. €€

Ananda
Sandyford Road, Dundrum Town Centre; www.anandarestaurant.ie
The intricate presentation and delicate spicing of the dishes – a wonderful *amuse-bouche* of lentil soup, a divine crab terrine and fabulous thalis – will

Temple Bar, Dublin

blow you away. Run by Atul Kochhar, chef-patron of the Michelin-starred Indian restaurant Benares in London. Excellent-value early-bird dinners. €€€€

Café en Seine
40 Dawson Street; www.cafeenseine.ie

Featuring a sensational indoor Parisian street garden, this Dawson Street favourite boasts a stunning Art Deco interior with three-storey atrium featuring intimate bars within bars. It's the trendy place to be. The casual, contemporary food is on offer all day and evening. €€

Chapter One
18–19 Parnell Square; www.chapteronerestaurant.com

One of Dublin's leading restaurants, this Michelin-starred establishment has a well-deserved reputation for superb, friendly service and outstanding classic/modern Irish cooking that showcases specialist Irish produce. A highlight is the Chef's Table; in particular the six-course menu. A meal here is a special treat (reserve well in advance). Lunch, and their renowned pre-theatre menu (dessert served after the theatre show), are great value. €€€€

Chez Max
1 Palace Street; www.chezmax.ie

An eternally popular bistro and epicerie close to Dublin Castle offering classic French dishes such as *moules frites* and *bœuf bourginon*

at exceptionally reasonable prices considering the high quality of food, cooking and table service. €€

Cornucopia
19–20 Wicklow Street; www.cornucopia.ie

Generations of Trinity students have refuelled at this vegetarian and vegan-friendly wholefood restaurant where the generous portions of tasty fare recall the best home-cooking. Excellent breakfast. €

Dunne & Crescenzi
14–16 South Frederick Street; www.dunneandcrescenzi.com

Billed as an authentic *'enoteca Italiana'*, this Italian restaurant and deli is renowned for its simple food and good wine. The prosciutto and mozzarella bars are a particular treat. €€

Ely Wine Bar
22 Ely Place; www.elywinebar.ie

Just off St Stephen's Green, this Georgian townhouse recalls the gracious Dublin of old. The list of more than 400 wines, many by the glass, is renowned. Traditional fare, including rare-breed pork sausages, steaks of organic and dry-aged beef, is largely sourced on the family farm in County Clare, while seafood is fresh from the Atlantic. A much bigger and contemporary Ely gastropub and a brasserie (see website) are in the same family. €€€

Los Chicanos
Eliot's Cash & Carry, 10 Camden Row, Saint Kevin's; www.loschicanos.ie

Hugo's Restaurant and Wine Bar

Native Irish chef Scott Holder brings the authentic flavours of Mexico to Dublin in the form of a very cool foodtruck. Order fish, chorizo, lamb, sweetpotato or cauliflower tacos, salsas and sides. Gluten free. It won't be long before there's a restaurant. Check location in advance. €

Market Bar
Fade Street; 01-613 9094; www.marketbar.ie
A gorgeous cavernous bar serving an exciting selection of tapas – Cajun sea trout, steamed mussels, beef stew – in small or large portions, with a good choice of wine. €€

Nanettis
22 Dawson Street; www.nannettis.ie
Nanetti's is a new Italian restuarant that is a bit of a crowd pleaser in a stylish space with brick walls and marble counters. Try the *fritto misto*, veal *saltimboca* or *gnocchi alla casa* with *tortino* or *tiramisu* to finish. Good wine list too. €€€

Yamamori South City
73 South Great George's Street;
www.yamamori.ie/southcity
The original incarnation of this excellent Japanese restaurant serving freshly prepared tempura, sushi, Japanese grill, noodles and ramen. Try the clay seafood hotpot or the good-value daily bento-box specials. Their North City branch (38/39 Ormond Quay Lower) and Izakaya Sake bar (12–13 South Great George's Street) are also worth a visit. €€

Around Dublin:
County Wicklow
The Happy Pear
Church Road, Greystones; www.thehappypear.ie
Located in a seaside village (beside the DART rail station) this is the home of the phenomenally successful and internationally renowned Happy Pear vegetarian café and veg shop, run by twin brothers Dave and Steve Flynn. Cooking courses also offered. €€€

Roundwood Inn
Roundwood (N11); 01-281 8107
Situated in Wicklow's highest village, en route to Glendalough, this seventeenth-century inn serves Irish-German fusion cuisine, with an emphasis on locally sourced meat and fish for dishes such as crab bisque, Wicklow trout, suckling pig and, in winter, roasted stuffed goose. €€€

Southeast: County Kilkenny
Ristorante Rinuccini
1 The Parade, Kilkenny City; www.rinuccini.com
Stylish, upmarket and always reliably good quality, this family-run Italian restaurant has been going for generations. Expect a menu featuring excellent meat and fish dishes alongside delicious fresh home-made pasta and risotto choices. Great desserts and lovely wine list, too. Booking advisable. €€€

Southeast: County Wexford
Beaches Restaurant and
La Marine Bistro
Kelly's Resort Hotel, Rosslare; www.kellys.ie

Seafood in Waterford

Family-run for more than 100 years, Beaches is formal fine dining and provides classic cooking. Menus change daily. La Marine offers relaxed, contemporary European-style menus with the odd Asian spin. €€-€€€

Harvest Room Restaurant
Dunbrody Country House Hotel, Arthurstown, New Ross; www.dunbrodyhouse.com

Talented TV chef Kevin Dundon serves some of Irish cuisine's most spectacular food at this small luxury hotel. The emphasis is on simple but imaginative combinations of fresh ingredients. The elaborate desserts are legendary. There's also the more informal (less pricey) Dundon's Champagne & Seafood Bar offering a selection of dishes in starter-size portions. €€€€

Southeast: County Waterford
Bodega
54 John Street, Waterford; www.bodegawaterford.com

Popular contemporary restaurant with an exciting menu. Start with sourdough and ricotta, then opt for monkfish scampi with pesto, steak or linguine… The changing menu doesn't disappoint. €€€

The Tannery
10 Quay Street, Dungarvan; www.tannery.ie

An old stone warehouse has been converted into a minimalist first-floor restaurant. Owner-chef Paul Flynn's cooking attracts food lovers from miles away. Start with crab crème brulée with pickled cucumber, followed by slow-cooked ox cheek. Closes annually for the last two weeks of January. €€€

Southwest: Cork city
Café Paradiso
16 Lancaster Quay, Western Road; www.cafeparadiso.ie

Owner-cook Denis Cotter has transformed the reputation of vegetarian cooking at his small but stylish restaurant. Even carnivores look forward to his imaginative, robustly spiced combinations of seasonal fare: in summer, perhaps, eggroll pancake of asparagus and Coolea cheese with a warm cherry tomato and fennel salsa; in autumn the signature pumpkin risotto. €€

Cornstore
40A Cornmarket Street; www.cornstorecork.com

A granite warehouse conversion in Cork's open-air market district over two floors, this is a buzzy dining experience in a Manhattan-style setting. Seafood is a speciality, as are their premium steaks, which include a Chateaubriand (fillet carved for two). €€€

Greenes
48 MacCurtain Street; www.greenesrestaurant.com

Turn off busy MacCurtain Street into a small cobblestoned alley for a pleasant surprise: at night this Victorian warehouse conversion is floodlit, and a natural waterfall runs down one wall; by day there are outdoor

Dessert at Café Paradiso, Cork

tables. Seafood is the speciality here, but meat and vegetarian food is also offered in Mediterranean-style dishes and Asian-influenced fusion cuisine. Afterwards you can consider checking out Cask (https://caskcork.com) next door, where award-winning cocktail consultant Andy Ferreira mixes elixirs to compliment creations by Greenes' chef Bryan McCarthy. €€

Isaacs Restaurant
48 MacCurtain Street; www.isaacsrestaurant.ie
Spacious converted warehouse. Relaxed, fun and vibrant. Good service, quality ingredients, and consistently excellent cooking delivered at a fair price. The food style is a mix of international and traditional, with good vegetarian options. €€

Jacob's Ladder
Water's Edge Hotel, Cobh;
www.watersedgehotel.ie
The real draw at Jacob's Ladder bar-restaurant is the mesmerising panoramic harbour view. This is complemented by a menu featuring the usual staples: expect soups, open sandwiches, pasta, burgers and steak a well as roast dinners. Unsurprisingly, there is a good selection of fresh fish and seafood dishes on offer. It's also a nice place to come for just a coffee or a cocktail. €€

Southwest: West Cork coast
Fishy Fishy Restaurant
Crowley's Pier, Kinsale; www.fishyfishy.ie

One of Ireland's leading seafood restaurants, Fishy Fishy occupies two floors of a substantial house in the town park. If you have never tried real scampi made from freshly caught prawns, this is the place to do it. The salads are really good with generous portions, and the warm seafood salad is an eternal lunchtime favourite. Shorter opening hours in winter. €€€

Mary Ann's
Castletownshend, Skibbereen; (028)-36146
Said to be one of the oldest bars in Ireland, this dream gastropub is hidden away in a picturesque fishing village. Packed in summer, with a large patio, it's even more charming in winter, when there might be only a few diners in the low-ceilinged bar. Daily specials include hot crab gratin or lobster thermidor, while the seafood platter is legendary. €€€

Southwest: the Ring of Kerry
Park Hotel Kenmare
Kenmare; www.parkkenmare.com
Kenmare is the foodie capital of southwest Ireland and the Park may just be the jewel in its crown. The hotel's elegant dining room, built in 1897 by the Great Southern Railway, is imposing but friendly. Food is light but flavoursome, featuring seafood and local specialities, such as Kerry lamb and Skeaghanore West Cork duck. The bar and lounge serve a lighter menu during the day perfect for lunchtime dining. €€€€

Park Hotel, Kenmare

QC's
Church Street, Cahirciveen; 066-947 2244
Known simply as QC's, this award-winning seafood restaurant is a culinary highlight of Kerry, and a destination in its own right. The menu features fish from their own fleet of trawlers, and local game in season. It's located at the western end of town on the main (N70) road. €€€

Southwest: the Dingle Peninsula

Ashe's Bar
Main Street, Dingle; www.ashesrestaurant.ie
Ashe's pioneered bar food locally, famously feeding the cast of *Ryan's Daughter* which was filmed locally in 1969. The pub is cosy, quirky and old fashioned, but the menu is bang up to date, with prawn tempura, oysters, rib-eye steak and squid salad. €€

The Chart House
The Mall, Dingle; https://thecharthousedingle.com
The bright red half-door of Jim McCarthy's stone-built cottage restaurant is the first thing you see when arriving into the quaint fishing town of Dingle. A favourite starter is local black pudding in filo pastry with apple and date chutney and hollandaise sauce. Pork is served with brandied apples, pan-fried brill with smoked bacon and rocket. Desserts are a highlight. Restricted opening off season. €€

West: Limerick city & Shannon

Maigue Restaurant
At the Dunraven Arms, Adare;

Moran's Oyster Cottage

www.dunravenhotel.com
Country house atmosphere and a fine-dining menu are the order of the day here. A big draw is the excellent roast rib of beef carved directly at the table. Smart attire is essential. The hotel's Hunters Bar offers a more casual menu and relaxed vibe. €€€

Old Lodge Gastro Pub
Shannon Springs Hotel, Ballycasey, Shannon; www.shannonspringshotel.com
This airy gastro pub with banquette seating serves up a selection of the usual favourites for lunch and dinner such as steak, chicken and fish mains and wraps with a few surprises on the side such as tapas and Thai curries. Order an Eton mess or apple crumble to finish. Children's menu available. Traditional Irish breakfasts cater to the early birds. €€

Sash Restaurant
1 Pery Square, Limerick; 061-402 402
This elegant hotel in a Georgian townhouse is close to the city centre overlooking the People's Park. The classy but informal Sash Restaurant is on the first floor and serves breakfast, lunch and dinner in cosy, convivial surroundings. €€

West: the Cliffs of Moher and the Burren
Linnanes Lobster Bar
New Quay, The Burren, County Clare; www.linnanesbar.com
For the freshest lobster, you can't beat Linnanes. This casual County Clare favourite offers stunning views of the crashing Atlantic surf and, as expected, serves up some of the best and freshest seafood you'll find anywhere in the country. Order with a pint of Guinness for the ultimate Irish experience. Reservations are essential and you can book online on their website. €€

Moran's Oyster Cottage
The Weir, Kilcolgan, County Galway; www.moransoystercottage.com
One of the quintessential West of Ireland experiences is a seafood feast at Moran's. The tiny thatched pub is 500 metres/yds off the N18 (signposted in Kilcolgan), beside a wide weir and the Moran family's oyster beds. The front bar has been preserved, but there is also a large restaurant behind. Local oysters are in season from September to April; in summer there's crab and lobster on the menu. €€

The Pier Head
The Quay, Kinvara, County Galway; www.pierheadkinvara.ie
A corner bar on The Quay, with plate-glass windows offering views of Dunguaire Castle and the evening sunset across the bay, The Pier Head is hugely popular with locals. Sample the excellent seafood – mussels, skate and lobster – and locally sourced steak on the short but impeccably prepared menu. €€

West: Galway city
Ard Bia Café
By Spanish Arch; www.ardbia.com
This compact, waterside stone warehouse, with bare wooden floors and quirky art on the walls, is an atmospheric spot for a casual meal, featuring local artisan food. Pricier meals are served in the upstairs restaurant in the evening. A nice breakfast and weekend brunch menu are also on offer. €€

The Kings Head Bistro
15 High Street; www.thekingshead.ie
Previously the Malthouse, the Kings Head Bistro is connected to the pub of the same name, which dates to 1649. Perfect for a casual bite to eat in a relaxed atmosphere, right in the centre of Galway. €€

McDonagh's Fish & Chip Bar
22 Quay Street; www.mcdonaghs.net.

A healthy beef dish

Enjoy, freshly cooked, traditional fish and chips at this long-established Galway institution. €

Sangria Tapas Restaurante
5 Buttermilk Walk (between Middle & Augustine Sts); www.sangriagalway.com
Sensational South American seafood and meat tapas in the heart of Galway City, created and infused with Latin flavour by head chef Byron Godoy. Renowned for lovely service and chilled atmosphere. Try the octopus and prawn ceviche. The same crew run a sister venue, The Bayview Restaurant, on Inishmore (the largest of the Aran Islands). €–€€

The Seafood Bar@Kirwan's
Kirwan's Lane; www.kirwanslane.ie
Kirwan's Lane is a quiet medieval alleyway off Galway's long main street, and the restaurant is a smart, contemporary space on two airy levels. The cuisine is contemporary Irish, specialising in seafood but with plenty of choice from meat to vegetarian dishes. €€€

West: Connemara
Leenane Hotel
Leenane, Co Mayo; www.leenanehotel.com
This venerable old hotel overlooking Killary Fjord serves bar food beside the open fire at lunchtime. In the evening the dining room is packed with savvy punters tucking into a great-value menu. This includes baked Killary Bay

salmon with lime *beurre blanc*, and rack of Connemara mountain lamb. €€

The Owenmore Restaurant
Ballynahinch Castle Hotel, Recess, Co Galway; www.ballynahinch-castle.com
It's not really a castle but rather a massive Victorian mansion with crenellations, set in romantic woodland on the banks of Ballynahinch River. The five-course set dinner menu offers a wide choice of classic dishes to choose from, including local game. Meals are also served in the bar. €€€€

West: Westport town
An Port Mór Restaurant
1 Brewery Place; www.anportmor.com
Proprietor-chef Frankie Mallon's forte is seafood, and here you can taste the best, fresh from Clew Bay. Try the scallops, or the crab cakes in a seaweed polenta, with a side of coffee, almond and black-pepper bread. €€€

La Fougère
Knockranny House Hotel and Spa; 098-28600; www.knockrannyhousehotel.ie
This Victorian-style hotel was built on an elevated site overlooking the town. The hotel dining room, La Fougère (The Fern) has views across the town to Croagh Patrick and Clew Bay, and creates a sense of occasion with its traditional table settings. The menus offer a wide choice of fine local produce, including Mayo mountain lamb and Clare Island salmon. The Brehon Bar also serves food,

A Limerick restaurant

as well as fancy drinks for those who've had enough of pints of porter. €€€€

Northwest: Sligo town

Hargadon Bros
4–5 O'Connell Street; www.hargadons.com
One of Ireland's great traditional pubs, its interior has changed very little since its opening back in 1864. The restaurant serves a simple menu of hearty fare, much of it organic and locally produced – from oysters to crab linguini, bangers and mash and the farmhouse cheese platter – at great prices. €

Montmartre
1 Market Yard, Caltragh;
www.montmartrerestaurant.ie
Montmartre's owner/chef is (unsurprisingly given the restaurant's name) French, and pleases locals and homesick French visitors alike with his traditional, well-executed menu. Children welcome. €€

The Venue
Strandhill; www.venuestrandhill.ie
Traditional and friendly, the Venue serves top-notch steak and seafood. Favourite dishes with regulars include the Lissadell mussels, crab claws and seafood chowder. €€

Northwest: Donegal town

The Harbour Restaurant & Bar
Quay St, Glebe
Family friendly, locally favoured steakhouse, which also offers hearty,

Dessert at James Street South

reliable and reasonably priced pizza, seafood and vegetarian options. €€

Olde Castle Bar and Red Hugh's Restaurant
Tirconnell Street; www.oldecastlebar.com
An old stone-built bar across the street from the town's famous castle serves great bar food at lunch, including Irish stew (lamb and root vegetables in broth). At night the upstairs restaurant has a great reputation for local seafood, from battered haddock to oysters and lobster. €€

Northern Ireland: Belfast

Coco
7–11 Linenhall Street; www.cocobelfast.com
Coco has gained a reputation as one of the best and coolest restaurants in the city. Owned by a

Hargadon Bros, Sligo town

talented local chef Jason More, the eclectic interior is complemented by a no-nonsense menu. ££

Deane's Deli + Bistro
44 Bedford Street; www.michaeldeane.ie
Deane's Deli is part of the restaurant empire of innovative Belfast chef Michael Deane. A relaxed café during the day, with fabulous cheese, meat and antipasti boards, it turns into an atmospheric 'vin-café' by night. The delicious food is locally sourced and cooked with a delicate touch. The fish specials – local hake with chorizo, or whole baked monkfish – are a must-try. ££

Ginger
6–8 Hope Street; www.gingerbistro.com
Young owner-chef Simon McCance cooks in a contemporary style, using locally-sourced ingredients. He aims to keep his menu simple and let the food do the talking and he delivers with gusto. In spite of its central location near the famous Crown Liquor Saloon, Ginger has the buzz and friendliness of a neighbourhood restaurant. £££

James Street South
21 James Street South;
www.jamesstreetsouth.co.uk
An exceptional and much-applauded restaurant offering an exciting and innovative menu, with top-class cooking with service to match. The charcoal grill offerings are really good and cater to vegetarians, too. Many regulars come here for the excellent steak and it's regularly voted as having the best Sunday roast in Belfast. Good value set-menus available throughout the week. £££

Mourne Seafood Bar
34–36 Bank Street; www.mourneseafood.com
One of the city's favourite restaurants, this seafood bar serves up the daily catch from the owners' beds in Carlingford Lough, and the ports of Annalong and Kilkeel in County Down. The Mourne seafood casserole is renowned. ££

Neill's Hill Brasserie
229 Upper Newtownards Road;
www.neillshill.com
Modern restaurant serving great wholesome favourites. Extensive menu of seafood and locally sourced meat, with daily specials on the blackboard, and consistently good cooking and service. ££

Town Square
45 Botanic Avenue;
www.townsquarebelfast.com
An award-winning head barista working with coffee beans that were recently voted Ireland's best make this place a magnet for caffeinds, but the food is amazing too. Under the umbrella of Crescent Townhouse Hotel – it's part café, part bar and part restaurant. Open daily and regular live music. ££

Mourne Seafood Bar, Belfast

Nightlife

Aside from Irish music, dancing and pubs, Ireland offers state-of-the-art theatres and concert venues. Some of the main venues are listed here.

The Irish will gladly pursue the *craic* for several hours until they find it. The two capitals and Cork, Galway, Limerick and Sligo all have thriving live music scenes; check the local papers for details or ask around, particularly in smaller towns. A local barperson will usually know which bar or venue has live sounds that evening. Impromptu music sessions, or even recitations of stories or poetry, are common.

In Dublin, the Button Factory (Curved Street; www.buttonfactory. ie) hosts an eclectic line-up of hip-hop, electro, dance and indie; for comedy, rock and folk, head to Vicar St (58–59 Thomas Street). Dublin's longest-running and best-loved rock venue is Whelans (25 Wexford Street; www.whelanslive.com). In Belfast, try The John Hewitt (51 Donegall Street; www.thejohnhewitt.com) for blues, jazz and folk, or Madden's Bar (74 Berry Street) for traditional Irish music.

Dublin

Abbey Theatre
Lower Abbey Street; www.abbeytheatre.ie
Founded in 1903 by W.B. Yeats and Lady Gregory, the Abbey rejuvenated Irish literature and culture. Ireland's national theatre still features many Irish classics in its programme. The Abbey's sister theatre, the Peacock, stages new work.

Gaiety Theatre
South King Street; www.gaietytheatre.ie
A fine Victorian building, recently restored, with a programme that includes opera, ballet, pantomime, musicals and serious drama.

Gate Theatre
1 Cavendish Row, Parnell Square;
www.gatetheatre.ie
Founded in 1928, the Gate stages the classics of European, Irish and American theatre by playwrights such as Samuel Beckett, Brian Friel and Arthur Miller.

Olympia Theatre
72 Dame Street; www.olympia.ie
One of the oldest theatres in Dublin, the Olympia was once a Victorian music hall; now it is used both as a theatre and as a venue for live bands.

Project Arts Centre
39 East Essex Street, Temple Bar;
www.projectartscentre.ie
Stages cutting-edge theatre, dance and music, as well as contemporary art exhibitions.

Samuel Beckett Theatre
Trinity College; www.tcd.ie/beckett-theatre

Live music in Belfast

The Beckett is based in the university that produced such dramatists as Goldsmith, Synge and Beckett himself, and is run in association with the university's Samuel Beckett Centre. It's a venue for both the Dublin Fringe and Dublin Theatre festivals.

Southwest: Cork city

Cork Opera House
Emmet Place; www.corkoperahouse.ie
Cork's principal theatre since the late nineteenth century offers drama, musicals, family shows, dance and comedy.

Everyman Palace
15 MacCurtain Street;
www.everymancork.com
This 650-seat late-Victorian theatre stages drama and musicals, and also hosts club nights.

Southwest: Tralee

Siamsa Tíre: National Folk Theatre of Ireland
Town Park, Tralee; www.siamsatire.com
The Irish rural tradition is celebrated here in song, dance and mime.

West: Limerick city

Lime Tree Theatre
Mary Immaculate College, Courtbrack Avenue; www.limetreetheatre.ie
A modern, 510-seat theatre that stages music, comedy, drama and traditional arts. Located on the campus of Mary Immaculate College.

West: Ennis

Glór Irish Music Centre
Causeway Link; www.glor.ie
A modern building with two auditoria. Irish music shows in summer; theatre and comedy for the rest of the year.

West: Galway city

Druid Theatre Company
Druid Lane Theatre, Druid Lane;
www.druidtheatre.com
One of Ireland's most successful repertory theatre companies presents a mix of new work and revivals in its refurbished 90-seat theatre. Other companies perform at the 400-seat Town Hall Theatre (Courthouse Square; www.tht.ie).

Northwest: Sligo town

Hawk's Well Theatre
Temple Street; www.hawkswell.com
A modern theatre that hosts touring and local shows; home of the annual W.B. Yeats International Summer School.

Northern Ireland: Belfast

Grand Opera House
Great Victoria Street; www.goh.co.uk
This glorious 1895 building is Belfast's biggest entertainment venue, staging drama, musicals, ballet and pantomime.

Lyric Theatre
Ridgeway Street; https://lyrictheatre.co.uk
Northern Ireland's only full-time producing theatre has an £18m state-of-the-art building on the banks of the River Lagan with a bar and café.

Abbey Theatre, Dublin

DIRECTORY NIGHTLIFE

The MAC
Hurst House, 18–19 Corporation Square; www.themaclive.com
A multi-discipline arts centre in Belfast's Cathedral Quarter with two theatres and three art galleries.

Waterfront Hall
2 Lanyon Place; www.waterfront.co.uk
A multi-purpose venue offering comedy, theatre, music and conferences, with two exhibition galleries.

Nightclubs

Dublin
Button Factory
Curved Street, Temple Bar, Dublin 2; www.buttonfactory.ie
Probably Dublin's best-known venue for exciting live music, from rock to dance and electro, frequented by music buffs as well as clubbers.

La Cave
28 South Anne Street, Dublin 2; www.lacavewinebar.com
Tiny, late-night venue which falls somewhere between a restaurant, wine bar and nightclub, although there's no dance floor as such. The Latino sounds and intimate atmosphere make this a favourite with an eclectic crowd wanting to kick back well into the wee small hours.

Copper Face Jacks
29–30 Harcourt Street, Dublin 2; http://copperfacejacks.ie

For when you don't feel like posing and just want to bop the night away to chart, dance and R&B. This hotspot has been Dublin's favourite nightclub since its inception in 1995.

Farrier & Draper
Powerscourt Townhouse Centre, South William St, Dublin 2; www.farrieranddraper.ie
Cool late-night destination for a style-conscious crowd to lounge in Georgian splendour. Great cocktails and amazing interiors in three bars spread over three levels with an Italian restaurant in the basement.

The George
89 South Great George's Street, Dublin 2; www.thegeorge.ie
Probably the city's most popular LGBTQ+ club. The George pub, from which the club takes its name, is a favourite meeting place among gay men. Stylish dress.

House
27 Lower Leeson Street, Dublin 2; www.housedublin.ie
Ultra-hip venue where everyone who's anyone in rock music, the media and modelling congregate. The dance floor is home to the young and beautiful. You probably already know to wear hip clothes.

Lillie's Bordello
Adam Court, Grafton Street, Dublin 2; www.lilliesbordello.ie

Grand Opera House, Belfast

One of the most exclusive clubs in town, and one that prides itself on its VIP lounge where high-profile party animals rub shoulders with fellow celebrities. Non-members are not guaranteed entry, but looking like a celeb can work wonders on the bouncers. Stylish clothes essential.

Octagon Bar at the Clarence Hotel
6–8 Wellington Quay, Dublin 2; www.theclarence.ie
This octagon-shaped, honey-coloured bar is the place to see and be seen in Dublin. The cocktails are world-class. Try the flavoured daiquiris or the delicious 'Bramble' (a gin-based cocktail).

Sugar Club
8 Lower Leeson Street, Dublin 2; www.thesugarclub.com
Live bands most nights are followed by DJ sets. The bar has one of the city's most extensive cocktail menus.

Vicar Street
58–59 Thomas Street, Dublin 8; 01-775 5800
A hugely successful music venue opposite Christchurch Cathedral, with seats for 1,050, or 1,500 standing, it is the place to catch live performances by big and up and coming names. Also has comedy nights.

The Wild Duck
17/20 Sycamore Street, Dublin 2; www.thewildduck.ie
Temple Bar's newest theatre, live music and fancy food venue, offering tasty tidbits and drinks, plus various forms of live entertainment from noon till late every day of the week.

The Workman's Club
10 Wellington Quay, Dublin 2; http://theworkmansclub.com/
This live music venue, with retro interiors, is spread over two floors and has played host to some legendary acts over the years. Right in the centre of Temple Bar beside the Clarence Hotel.

Belfast
Limelight
17 Ormeau Avenue; www.limelightbelfast.com
One of Belfast's longest established and best venues for live music and club nights.

Northern Whig
2 Bridge Street; www.thenorthernwhig.com
Housed in what was once an old Belfast newspaper office. Don't miss the three granite statues of socialist workers rescued from Soviet-era Prague after the fall of communism. The bar, restaurant and nightclub are usually heaving on weekends.

Robinson's
38–40 Great Victoria Street; www.robinsonsbar.co.uk
This complex, next to the Crown, includes the perennially popular Fibber Magee's pub, the more upmarket BT1, and Roxy, home to dance nights and live music. Check out original memorabilia from the Titanic on the ground floor of Robinson's.

Belfast's Waterfront Hall

Essentials

Age restrictions

The age of consent is 17. At 17 you can apply for a driver's licence. The legal drinking age is 18, but some pubs will only serve those over 21 carrying photo ID. You must be 18 to buy cigarettes and tobacco. In the Republic of Ireland, under 18s are not allowed on premises that serve alcohol after 9.30pm.

Budgeting

The cost of a pint of draught beer in the Republic starts from €5.50; wine from about €6 for 175ml. Beer costs approximately €7 a pint in Dublin, and wine about €7-8 a glass, but it could be more in a fashionable bar and up to twice as much in a five-star hotel.

A main course at a budget restaurant costs on average €15, at a moderate restaurant €18–28 and at an expensive one, over €30.

A double room with breakfast costs about €70–100 at a B&B or guesthouse, €120–200 at a moderate hotel and €250-plus at an expensive hotel.

Restaurant and hotel prices in Northern Ireland are roughly comparable, although groceries and other products are often cheaper in Northern Ireland than in the Republic.

A taxi from Dublin airport to the city centre costs €30. A single bus ticket in Dublin or Cork costs around €1.30, and a Dublin tram (Luas) ticket costs from €1.70. These are all cheaper with a Leap card (contactless smart card). 'Leap Visitor Cards' can be bought to cover 1/3/7 days.

Admission to national museums in both the Republic and Northern Ireland is free. Charges for other heritage attractions vary from €3–12 and up. A Heritage Card gives free admission to over 90 national sights and monuments (www.heritageireland.ie) and is worthwhile if you plan to see lots. From Dublin Tourism, you can buy a pass that gives free admission to 25 sights plus other concessions (www.dublinpass.com).

Children

The Irish love children. They are usually welcome at hotels and B&Bs, most of which can supply special cots or babysitting services. Many hotels allow children to stay in their parents' room at no extra charge; check when booking. Some of the grander country houses will only accept children over 12.

Most restaurants can supply highchairs and a children's menu. Kids are generally welcome in pubs up to about 7pm (and by law under 18s must be gone by 9.30pm), but this is at the discretion of the landlord.

Playing by St Patrick's in Dublin

During holiday periods, there are plenty of child-oriented activities organised by museums, local festivals and outdoor centres; tourist offices will have full details.

Clothing

You can safely leave your formal clothes at home, unless you are going to the Wexford Festival Opera. Smart-casual is acceptable just about everywhere. Because of the unpredictability of the weather, pack an umbrella, some rainproof clothing and a warm sweater, even in summer. But bring sun cream as well; it does shine sometimes.

Crime and safety

While rural Ireland is a low-risk area for crime, hired vehicles are easy targets for criminals, and thefts from cars are commonplace in Dublin, other major towns and cities, and in the car parks of visitor attractions. Never leave anything visible in your car, even if you are only leaving it briefly. Be careful when withdrawing money from ATMs, and shield your PIN number. Beware of pickpockets in crowded places. In central Dublin ask your hotel whether it is safe to walk home in the dark (take particular care around the Lower Gardiner Street and Connolly Station). It is sensible to keep a copy of your passport in case of theft.

Victims of crime in the Republic should contact Irish Tourist Assistance Service, Pearse Garda Station, Dublin 2; tel: 1890-365 700.

Customs

Visitors of all nationalities entering or leaving the EU via Ireland or Northern Ireland must declare on arrival or departure sums of cash above €10,000.

Visitors within the EU may import the following goods, provided they were purchased within the EU and are for personal use: 800 cigarettes, 400 cigarillos, 200 cigars, 1kg tobacco, 10 litres spirits, 20 litres fortified wines, 90 litres wine, 110 litres beer.

From outside the EU you may import duty-free: 200 cigarettes or the tobacco equivalent, 4 litres of wine or 1 litre of spirits, and other goods to the value of €430 per person.

For details of restricted goods, see www.revenue.ie.

Non-EU visitors can claim back sales taxes on purchases made in the Republic. Participating stores have a 'Tax Free Shopping' sign in the window. If the item is priced at €2000 or more, you must present the tax refund documentation and the goods to customs on departure. Some airports will refund you on the spot; otherwise, mail the validated document back to the store and a refund will be issued. The VAT rate on most items is 23 percent.

Disabled travellers

Ireland is still introducing facilities such as ramps and accessible toilets

Ha'Penny Bridge, Dublin

Looking out over the Cliffs of Moher

for people with disabilities. Public transport in Dublin is now excellent but some parts of the country lag behind. However, visitors with disabilities often find that people's helpfulness makes up for the lack of amenities.

In the Republic, the key organisation for practical information, wheelchair rental and parking permits is the Irish Wheelchair Association (Áras Chúchulainn, Blackheath Drive, Clontarf, Dublin; tel: 01-818 6400). The official government body is the National Disability Authority (25 Clyde Road, Ballsbridge, Dublin 4; www.nda.ie). The Head Office of Fáilte Ireland (88-95 Amiens St, Dublin 1; www.failteireland.ie) can advise on attractions and accommodation suitable for disabled visitors.

In Northern Ireland, Disability Action (Portside Business Park, 189 Airport Road West, Belfast; www.disability action.org) offers practical advice.

Electricity

220 volts AC (50 cycles) is standard. Hotels usually have dual 220/110 voltage sockets for electric razors only. Most sockets require a 3-pin plug; visitors may need an adaptor.

Embassies and consulates

Dublin
Australia. Fitzwilton House, Wilton Terrace, Dublin 2; www.ireland.embassy.gov.au.

Britain. 29 Merrion Road, Dublin 4; www.britishembassy inireland.fco.gov.uk.
Canada. 7–8 Wilton Terrace, Dublin 2; www.canada.ie.
US. 42 Elgin Road, Dublin 4; https://ie.usembassy.gov.

Belfast
American Consulate General. Danesfort House, 223 Stranmillis Road, Belfast BT9 5GR; https://uk.us embassy.gov/embassy-consulates/belfast.

Emergencies

In an emergency, dial 999 (or 112, a number that you can also text).

Etiquette

The Irish love a chat, and they expect visitors to respond in kind. Strike up a conversation with the person sitting next to you at the bar or on the bus and be prepared to launch into either your or their life story. Pub etiquette is based on good manners: if somebody buys you a drink, buy one back. Discussions about politics and/or religion can be sensitive in the north. Avoid telling people what's wrong with their country (e.g. the roads, the signposts, the high cost of everything); they know already.

Green issues

Ireland has an active Green Party (www.greenparty.ie) and, after a slow start, it has become a leading nation in cutting down on waste. It imposed

Slieve League cliffs in County Donegal

a levy on plastic bags in supermarkets way back in 2002 and is ranked seventh in the EU for recycling and recovery of packaging. Renewable energy is a growing industry; in 2022, wind-generated power provided 47 percent of Ireland's renewable electricity. Many of Ireland's smaller farms are now managed under REPs (Rural Environment Protection Scheme), to encourage wildlife and biological diversity. But overuse of fertilizer in farming and forestry has led to pollution of lakes and rivers.

For the latest, visit www.friendsof theirishenvironment.org.

Health

Medical insurance is advisable for all visitors. However, visitors from EU countries are entitled to medical treatment in the Republic and Northern Ireland under reciprocal arrangements.

Visitors from EU states should obtain a European Health Insurance Card (EHIC), which entitles the holder to treatment through the public health system. If hospital treatment is necessary, this will be given free on a public ward. At the time of writing, UK visitors can receive medically necessary treatment (or, in an emergency, hospital treatment) on presentation of some form of ID (eg a driving licence) under the health agreement in place. Some treatment may require payment.

Hospitals and pharmacies

Dublin. St Vincent's University Hospital, Merrion Road, Dublin 4; www.stvincents.ie.
Hickey's Pharmacy, 55 Lower O'Connell Street; www.hickeys pharmacies.ie. Also branches on Grafton St and Henry St.
McCabe's Late Night Pharmacy, Dundrum Town Centre; www.mccabespharmacy.com. Open until 11pm 7 nights a week
Belfast. Belfast City Hospital, 51 Lisburn Road; www.belfasttrust.hscni.net
Urban Pharmacy, 56 Dublin Road, BT2 7HN; T 028-9024 6336.

Hours and holidays

Shops and department stores usually open Mon–Sat 9.30am–6 or 7pm and Sun noon–6pm. In smaller towns some shops close for lunch between 1pm and 2pm. Supermarkets and convenience stores generally open daily until 9pm. Post offices open Mon–Fri 9am–5.30pm and Sat 9am–1pm. Government offices are open Mon–Fri 9am–5pm.

Museums and other tourist sights are often closed on Monday, and outside Dublin and Belfast most have restricted opening hours between November and Easter or late May.

In hotels and B&Bs, breakfast is generally served from 8–10am, and in restaurants and pubs until noon. Restaurants and pubs generally serve lunch between 12.30 and 2.30pm, and dinner from 6 to 9.30pm.

Shopping in Dublin

Public holidays

1 Jan: New Year's Day
17 Mar: St Patrick's Day
Mar/Apr: Good Fri and Easter Mon
1st Mon May: Early
May Bank Holiday
Last Mon May: Bank Holiday (NI)
1st Mon June: Bank Holiday (RoI)
12 July: Bank Holiday (NI)
1st Mon Aug: Bank Holiday (RoI)
Last Mon Aug: Bank Holiday (NI)
Last Mon Oct: Bank Holiday (RoI)
25 Dec: Christmas Day
26 Dec: St Stephen's Day
(RoI) Boxing Day (NI)

Internet facilities

Wi-fi is widely available free in cafés, bars and public areas of hotels.

LGBTQ+

There should be no major problems for gay and lesbian travellers in Ireland. Be as safety conscious as you would in any foreign city or country. Openly gay couples may attract unwanted attention in small-town pubs, but the country has become a lot more progressive in its attitudes in recent years.

Information on LGBTQ+-friendly bars and clubs, accommodation, advice and contacts can be found through the following organisations:
Dublin. Outhouse, 51 Capel Street; www.outhouse.ie.
Cork. Cork Gay Project, 4 South Terrace; www.gayproject.ie.

West of the Shannon. Out West Ireland, PO Box 58, Castlebar, County Mayo; www.outwest.ie.
Belfast. Queer Space, 3rd Floor, Belfast LGBT Centre, 28–31 Waring Street, BT1 2DX; www.queerspace.org.uk.

Maps

Cyclists and walkers may want small-scale maps; these can be bought locally from bookshops, newsagents and tourist offices. The latter usually also offer a free town and surrounding area map.

Media

Print media. *The Irish Times* is Ireland's newspaper of record, with good coverage of foreign news, arts and business. The *Irish Independent* is published daily in Dublin, and the *Irish Examiner* in Cork. Two morning papers are published in Belfast, the *Belfast Newsletter* and *Irish News*. Each city also publishes an evening paper, useful for entertainment listings.
Television and radio. In the Republic RTÉ (www.rte.ie) broadcasts three channels including Irish-language TG4 (www.tg4.ie). Most UK channels are available on satellite or cable TV, which is widespread in hotels and B&Bs (confirm on booking). In Northern Ireland, the BBC Northern Ireland (www.bbc.com/northernireland) includes local coverage.

In the Republic, RTÉ1 is the main radio station for news, current affairs and drama, 2FM plays pop music and Lyric FM is for lovers of

Letter box with the modern Irish Gaelic name for Dublin

classical music. National commercial radio stations Newstalk and Today FM are very popular. There are also a number of independent local radio stations, such as Shannonside FM in the mid-west. In Northern Ireland the commercial-free BBC Radio Ulster has full local coverage, as do Downtown Radio and Cool FM.

Money

Currency. The Republic of Ireland is in the Eurozone. Banknotes come in denominations of €5, €10, €20, €50, €100, €200 and €500, coins in denominations of 1, 2, 5, 10, 20 and 50 cents, €1 and €2. Most places will round off the price if paying in cash so don't expect change of 2 cent for example. You also will not be able to use the lower denominations in machines such as at carparks. In Northern Ireland, the British pound (£) is the standard currency, although most traders in border areas are prepared to accept euros. Banknotes: £5, £10, £20 and £50; coins: 1p, 2p, 5p, 10p, 20p, 50p, £1 and £2.

Banking hours. Banks are open Mon–Fri 10am–4pm, with one day late opening until 5pm (Thu in Dublin). AIB on Grafton St is open Mon–Fri 8am–7pm (Thu until 9pm) and Sat–Sun 10am–6pm. Smaller town banks may close for lunch from 12.30–1.30pm.

Cash machines. Nearly all banks have 24-hour cash machines (ATMs), but not all towns have banks. In smaller places, cash machines can be found in convenience stores. Check with your bank before leaving home to confirm that your bankcard will work in Ireland.

Credit cards. The most widely accepted cards are Visa and Mastercard, followed by American Express. Many but not all guesthouses and B&Bs take credit cards; check in advance.

Tipping. Tipping is not expected in bars, except in lounge bars where drinks are brought to your table. It is usual to give at least a 10 percent tip to waiting staff. Round taxi fares to the nearest euro or pound, and porters are given about €1 or £1 a bag.

Police

The Republic is policed by the Garda Síochána (Guardians of the Peace), and Northern Ireland by the Police Service of Northern Ireland (PSNI). In an emergency, dial 999; 112 is also used in the Republic.

Post

Postage stamps are sold by post offices, newsagents and general stores. Letters and postcards cost €1.35 to send within the Republic and €2.20 to the UK, mainland Europe and North America; they cost £1.10 within the UK, £3.25 to Europe and more for the rest of the world (first class). In the Republic most letterboxes are pillar-shaped and are painted green; in Northern

Dublin bus tours

Ireland the letterboxes are red. Note that Republic of Ireland stamps may not be used on mail posted in Northern Ireland and vice versa.

Post offices. Hours are generally Mon–Fri 9am–5.30pm and Sat 9am–1pm. The General Post Offices in the two capitals are at O'Connell Street, Dublin (01-705 7000) and 12/16 Bridge Street, Belfast (0845-611 2970).

Smoking

Smoking is banned in all workplaces, including taxis, bars, restaurants and nightclubs. Elaborate sheltered outdoor smoking areas are provided by many pubs and clubs.

Telephones

The international dialling code for the Republic of Ireland is 353. Northern Ireland's is 44. If you are calling the North from the Republic, just substitute the code 028 with 048, rather than using the international dialling code.

There are several telecommunications companies operating in Ireland, the largest one being Eir (www.eir.ie). Public telephones mainly use phone cards, which are widely available from newsagents and supermarkets. Phone boxes are gradually disappearing, as the mobile phone gains dominance. International calls can be dialled direct from private phones, or dial

1901 for customer service. For directory enquiries dial 11811, for international directory enquiries 11818. The long-distance services of BT Ireland, AT&T, Sprint and MCI are also available.

Services in Northern Ireland are operated by British Telecom (www.bt.com); dial 100 for the operator.

Mobile (cell) phones. Only mobiles with GSM will work in Ireland. If your phone is non-GSM, consult with your provider before travelling. It may be cheaper to buy a local SIM card and top up with prepaid calls. Local providers include GoMo, 3, Meteor, Tesco Mobile and Virgin Mobile Ireland. If you are coming from the UK, your mobile should work in Northern Ireland, but you will need international roaming in the Republic.

Time zones

Ireland follows Greenwich Mean Time. In spring, the clock moves one hour ahead for Summer Time; in autumn it moves back to GMT. At noon – according to GMT – it is 4am in Los Angeles, 7am in New York, 1pm in western Europe, 8pm in Singapore, 10pm in Sydney and midnight in New Zealand.

Tourist information

Fáilte Ireland Dublin Head Office. 88–95 Amiens Street; 1800 242 473; www.failteireland.

Walking to the beach at Lahinch, County Clare

ie (For tourist information, 0800 313 4000 in the UK.)
Dublin Tourism Centre. Suffolk Street (near Grafton Street); 01-605 7700.
Regional offices. Local tourist offices can be found throughout Ireland. A number are mentioned in the tours in this guide.
Northern Ireland Tourist Board. 59 North Street, Belfast BT1 1NB; www.discovernorthernireland.com.

Transport

Passengers should check government Covid-19 restrictions before travelling.

Arrival by air

There are flights from Britain and Europe to Belfast, Dublin, Cork and Shannon airports, with more than thirty airlines flying from over seventy destinations. There are also frequent flights from British airports to regional airports in Kerry, Galway and Knock.

Aer Lingus (www.aerlingus. com), British Airways (www.british airways.com), easyJet (www.easy jet.com) and Ryanair (www.ryan air.com) fly to Britain.

There are direct flights from the US to Dublin and Shannon airports and Belfast International Airports with Aer Lingus (www.aerlingus. com), American Airlines (www.aa. com), United (www.united.com), Delta Airlines (www.delta.com) and US Airways (www.usairways.com).

Airport to city

Republic. There is a regular bus service from **Dublin Airport** (www.dublin airport.com) to the main bus station in the city centre (30 min), while Aircoach (www.aircoach.ie) departs every 10–20 minutes for various city locations. The bus from **Cork Airport** (www.corkairport.com) to the city takes about 10 minutes. From **Shannon Airport** (www.shannonairport.com) there is a regular bus service to Limerick city (30 min) and other main cities.

A **taxi** from the airport to the city centre should cost approximately €35-40 in Dublin, €20 in Cork and €40-55 in Shannon (to Limerick).
Northern Ireland. There are two major airports: **Belfast International**, (www.belfastairport.com) a 30-minute bus ride from town or about £38 by taxi, and **George Best Airport** (www. belfastcityairport.com), a short bus or taxi ride from the town centre. For more information on access to and from airports see www.discoverireland.com.

Arrival by sea

Ireland has five main ferry ports; Republic: Cork, Dublin, and Rosslare (County Wexford); Northern Ireland: Belfast and Larne (County Antrim). For details of operators and routes, see www.discoverireland.com.

Public transport in Ireland

Outside Dublin in the Republic, public transport can be limited. **Bus**

Cycling in Wicklow

Éireann (www.buseireann.ie) serves provincial Ireland with both local and direct express services. Its Expressway timetable (available online) is essential if you plan to travel by bus, and its Open Road passes allow flexible cross-country travel. Dublin's main bus station (Busáras) is on Store Street.

Iarnród Éireann (Irish Rail (www.irishrail.ie) runs rail services from Connolly, Pearse Street and Heuston stations to the main towns in Ireland, including Belfast. Fares are reasonable (e.g. Dublin–Cork one way: €21, Dublin–Galway one way: €17.99). Irish Rail also has a limited number of cut-price tickets available online.

The Republic is one of twenty-one countries in which you can use the global Eurailpass (www.eurail.com).

For details on public transport by bus and rail in Northern Ireland (and the Metro bus company in Belfast), visit www.translink.co.uk.

Public transport in Dublin

Dublin Bus (www.dublinbus.ie) has an extensive network within the greater Dublin area, with priority bus lanes ensuring progress through the often gridlocked traffic. Dublin Bus requires exact change to be given and will not accept notes or card payments other than the Leap card.

The bus network is supplemented by the **Luas** tram system (www.luas.ie). The Cross-City line takes passengers through the heart of Dublin, from St Stephen's Green right to the top of O'Connell Street and out into the suburbs. Purchase of a one-, seven- or 30-day Flexi ticket allows for unlimited travel on the Luas. Leap cards are valid for Dublin Bus and the Luas, widely available from newsagents, and will give the best value. For ticket costs, see Budgeting.

The **DART** (www.irishrail.ie), a rapid transit railway, runs from the city centre along the coast from Howth in the north to Greystones in the south.

Taxis

There are metered taxis in Belfast, Cork, Dublin, Galway and Limerick. In other areas, fares should be agreed beforehand. Taxis are usually found at ranks in central locations, or booked by phone, and do not usually cruise the streets. **NRC Taxis** (www.nrc.ie) is one of the biggest Dublin companies.

Driving

Outside the cities, Irish roads are still among the least congested in Europe, although it is hard to believe this when you are stuck in a traffic jam in Dublin's ever-expanding suburbs. **Rules of the road**. Drive on the left on both sides of the border. All passengers must wear seat belts. Drink driving laws are strict, and it is an offence to drive with a concentration of alcohol exceeding 50mg per 100ml of blood.

Dublin cabs

Remember that in the Republic speed limit signs are in kilometres. The limit is 50km/h (31mph) in urban areas, 80km/h (50mph) on non-national roads, 100km/h (62mph) on national routes (green signposts) and 120km/h (75mph) on motorways. On-the-spot fines can be issued for speeding offences.

In Northern Ireland, the limit in urban areas is 30mph (48km/h), on country roads 60mph (96km/h), and 70mph (113km/h) on motorways and dual-carriageway trunk roads.

Tolls. There are toll charges for using the M50 Dublin orbital motorway, M3 south and north bound and the M1 northern motorway, the Dublin Port tunnel, Limerick tunnel, the Waterford bypass and some sections of rural motorway. Visit www.eflow.ie for information on barrier-free tolling.

Car hire. Be sure to book in advance for July and August. Car hire is expensive in Ireland, and advance booking as part of a fly-drive or train-ferry-drive package often leads to a better deal, as does booking online. Drivers under 25 and over 70 may have to pay a higher rate. Most companies will not rent cars to people over 76. If you intend to drive across the border, inform your rental company beforehand to check that you are fully insured. Car hire companies usually cover the motorway toll fees but check first.

Local and international car hire companies in both the Republic and Northern Ireland are listed on www.irelandcarhire.com.

Visas and passports

UK citizens do not require a passport to enter Ireland at present, but most carriers by air or sea ask for photographic ID, usually either a passport or driving licence. Check with the individual company before travelling, however, as this may change post-Brexit.

Non-UK nationals must have a valid passport. EU nationals and travellers from the US, Canada, Australia, New Zealand and South Africa are simply required to show a passport. Visitors of all other nationalities should contact their local Irish embassy or consulate before travelling to the Republic, or their British Embassy, High Commission or Consular Office before travelling to Northern Ireland.

Websites

www.ireland.com – the official tourism website of Failte Ireland.
www.discovernorthernireland.com – detailed information on the North.
www.entertainment.ie – for theatre, cinema, club and festival listings.
www.bandbireland.com – accommodation reservation network of B&B Ireland.
www.airbnb.co.uk/a/Ireland – Airbnb in Ireland.
www.hostels-ireland.com – Tourist Board-approved holiday hostels.
www.met.ie – for the latest forecast.

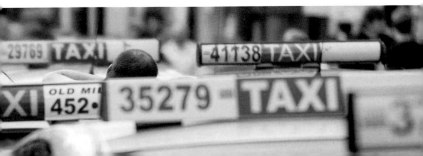

Books and Film

Books

Irish classics

Gulliver's Travels by Jonathan Swift (1667–1745). The Dean of Dublin's St Patrick's Cathedral was also a great satirist; this book is a savage indictment of mankind's folly.

Castle Rackrent by Maria Edgeworth (1768–1849). Published in 1800, Edgeworth's novel uses pointed humour to question Anglo-Irish identity and absentee landlords.

The Complete Works of Oscar Wilde (1854–1900). Besides his sparkling drawing room comedies, Wilde also wrote poetry, essays, charming children's stories and a novel.

Dracula by Bram Stoker (1847–1912). The most famous novel of Dublin-born Stoker's large output.

The Playboy of the Western World by J.M. Synge (1871–1909). The masterpiece of a multi-faceted writer who invented a new language using the poetry inherent in the Irish vernacular. Its earthy realism caused riots at its Abbey premiere.

Portrait of the Artist as a Young Man; Dubliners; Ulysses by James Joyce (1882–1941). His coming-of-age novel and the collection of Dublin stories will help you decide whether to tackle his magnum opus, *Ulysses*.

Pygmalion by George Bernard Shaw (1856–1950). The most famous work by the playwright credited with revolutionising comedic drama was later turned into the Broadway musical *My Fair Lady*.

Shadow of a Gunman; Juno and the Paycock; The Plough and the Stars by Sean O'Casey (1880–1964). His trilogy of tragicomedies is set in the Dublin tenements.

The Táin translated by Thomas Kinsella. An ancient Irish epic set in 1st-century pre-Christian age of Ireland, telling the tale of the Ulster hero Cú Chulainn during a war with Connacht.

The Vicar of Wakefield by Oliver Goldsmith (1728–74). A graduate of Trinity College, Dublin, who achieved fame for his work in London.

Essential contemporary fiction and poetry fiction

More Pricks than Kicks by Samuel Beckett. People are often surprised at how funny the Nobel Laureate's first story collection is.

Murphy by Samuel Beckett. Aspiring authors may be encouraged to know that this comic first novel was rejected by 41 publishers.

The Third Policeman and At Swim-Two-Birds by Flann O'Brien. Metafiction masterpieces by the modernist maestro of absurdist humour, real name Brian O'Nolan.

Listowel Writers' Week festival

An Old Woman's Reflections by Peig Sayers. Memoir written in Irish about life on the Great Blasket Island.

The Islandman by Tomás O Crohan. Vivid memoir of a Great Blasket Island farmer-fisherman, written originally in Irish.

The Ginger Man by J.P. Donleavy. Hilarious, account of post-war Dublin, as seen by a hard-living American.

Langrishe, Go Down by Aidan Higgins. The last great Irish 'big house' novel, chronicling its decline.

The Country Girls; A Fanatic Heart: Selected Stories, Saints and Sinners by Edna O'Brien. Her first novel is a witty picture of Dublin in the 1950s.

Troubles by J.G. Farrell. Wry, atmospheric account of sitting out the Civil War in a crumbling hotel.

The Book of Evidence and *The Sea* by John Banville. The first is a disturbing story of a Dublin murderer while his 2005 Booker Prize-winner is a tender account of lost love.

The South by Colm Tóibín. His first novel about an Irishwoman's love affair with Spain remains one of his best.

Collected Short Stories by William Trevor. Set in both England and Ireland, among the plain people. Trevor is a master of the quiet epiphany.

Creatures of the Earth: New and Selected Stories by John McGahern. One of the most understated and highly rated chroniclers of rural Ireland.

There are Little Kingdoms; Dark Lies the Island by Kevin Barry.

Barry uses anarchic comedy to skewer the absurdities of post-Celtic Tiger rural Ireland.

A Star Called Henry by Roddy Doyle. The finest book by the author of *The Commitments*, *The Snapper*, *The Van* and the Booker-Prize winning *Paddy Clarke Ha Ha Ha* is set amid the violent upheaval of the 1916–21 period.

All Names Have Been Changed by Claire Kilroy. A wry look at 1980s Ireland and its literary culture.

Milkman by Anna Burns. Disturbing, stylistically unique story of sexual, social and cultural coercement set in Derry. It won the 2018 Booker Prize for Fiction.

Poetry

Penguin Book of Contemporary Irish Poetry edited by Peter Fallon and Derek Mahon. Well-balanced selection of today's poets.

The Complete Works of W.B. Yeats (1865–1939). Winner of the 1923 Nobel Prize for Literature.

Collected Poems by Louis MacNeice. A major 20th-century poet, born in Ulster.

Collected Poems by Patrick Kavanagh (1904–67). Containing classics such as 'The Great Hunger' and 'On Raglan Road', which has been turned into a song performed by artists including Van Morrison, Luke Kelly, Dire Straits, Billy Bragg and Sinéad O'Connor.

Collected Poems and *Finders Keepers* by Seamus Heaney. Superbly crafted lyric poems, and a collection of his incisive literary essays and lectures.

W.B. Yeats' Nobel statue in Sligo Town

Collected Poems by Derek Mahon. A major 20th-century poet in the metaphysical mode.

Collected Poems by Michael Longley. At his best, his perceptive lyrics, often nature-inspired, can stand beside fellow Ulster poets, Heaney and Mahon.

A Snail in My Prime by Paul Durcan. Popular poet, known for his humour.

History

Luck and the Irish: A Brief History of Change, 1970–2000; Modern Ireland 1600–1972 by Roy Foster. Readable academic Irish history with many new insights.

The Story of Ireland: In Search of a New National Memory by Neil Hegarty. A fresh look at Irish history.

Ireland – A History by Robert Kee. Readable illustrated history, good on disentangling the Troubles.

How the Irish Saved Civilization by Thomas Cahill. A humorous look at Irish achievements down the years, with a serious core.

The Great Hunger: Ireland 1845–1849 by Cecil Woodham Smith. The classic account of the Famine.

Biography

James Joyce by Richard Ellman. One of the finest literary biographies.

W.B. Yeats, a Life by R.F. Foster. Definitive two-volume life of the poet.

Damned to Fame: A Life of Samuel Beckett by James Knowlson. The official biography.

Michael Collins by Tim Pat Coogan. The life of the pro-Treaty politician on which Neil Jordan's 1996 film was based.

Memoirs and journalism

Angela's Ashes by Frank McCourt. Bestselling account of a miserable childhood in Limerick.

Are You Somebody by Nuala O'Faolain. The late author's collected journalism is admirably candid about her problems with alcohol and relationships.

Borstal Boy by Brendan Behan. Autobiographical account of a three-year stint in a juvenile correction unit by a 16-year-old Behan – who would go on to be a celebrated playwright, poet and writer (*The Quare Fellow, The Hostage*).

My Left Foot and *Down All the Days* by Christy Brown. Lyrical autobiographical accounts of growing up Dublin by an author, painter and poet with cerebral palsy. The latter was turned into an Academy Award-winning film starring Daniel Day-Lewis as Brown in 1989.

To School Through the Fields by Alice Taylor. A simple account of a rural childhood in the 1940s.

Films

The Quiet Man (1952). Directed by John Ford and starring John Wayne and Maureen O'Hara, this whimsical Hollywood portrayal of Ireland – filmed in Cong, County Mayo – appealed to the huge Irish-American audience. The Irish, who were in reality facing hardship and chronic emigration, didn't

Dublin Writers Museum bookshop

object to such a portrayal: indeed, they built a tourist industry on it.

The Dead (1987). Veteran Hollywood director John Huston, who came of Irish stock and had a home in Ireland, captured the country's streak of Chekovian melancholy in his last film, adapted from a classic short story by James Joyce.

The Crying Game (1992). Neil Jordan explores the Troubles in Northern Ireland and the conflict's impact on a complicated web of human relationships. An IRA member starts a romance with the girlfriend of a British soldier, leading to unexpected consequences.

The Magdalene Sisters (2002). Peter Mullan's critically acclaimed film tells the story of the 30,000 young girls who were sent to live-in convent laundries as a punishment for having premarital sex or becoming pregnant out of wedlock. These sadistic labour camps finally closed in the 1990s.

Mickybo and Me (2004). Northern Irish comedy based on the stage play *Mojo Mickybo* by Owen McCafferty. Two young boys – one Catholic and one Protestant – become friends in the 1970s against the backdrop of the Troubles, sharing an obsession with *Butch Cassidy and the Sundance Kid*.

The Wind That Shakes the Barley (2006). The best film about the Irish Civil War by Ken Loach. Set in 1920 and filmed in rural Cork. Starring Cillian Murphy.

Once (2007). This musical romance, funded by the Irish Film Board, explores the touching relationship between an Irish busker and a Czech musician. Won an Oscar for Best Song.

Garage (2007). Lenny Abrahamson heart-wrenching story of a lonely garage attendant in a country town and won a prize at the Cannes Film Festival.

The Guard (2011). A cop comedy film written and directed by John Michael McDonagh, starring Brendan Gleeson, Don Cheadle, Mark Strong and Liam Cunningham.

Song of the Sea (2014). Animated film that sees a young boy and his mute sister Saoirse experience many adventures referencing Irish Celtic folk stories.

Brooklyn (2015). Film based on Colm Tóibín's novel of the same name, about a young Irish girl who immigrates to Brooklyn from Enniscorthy in the 1950s.

Sing Street (2016). Coming-of-age comedy-drama written and directed by John Carney. Ferdia Walsh-Peelo plays Conor, a boy who finds escapism from his family by forming a band.

Herself (2020). Tear-jerker drama about a woman who self-builds a home for her family after escaping an abusive husband. Directed by Phyllida Lloyd.

An Cailín Ciúin (2021). (*The Quiet Girl)* was the first Irish language film to be nominated for an Oscar tells the moving story of a young girl whose life is transformed after spending a summer with her relatives.

An Cailín Ciúin

About This Book

CREDITS

The Pocket Rough Guide Walks & Tours series helps you discover the world's most exciting destinations through expert-curated itineraries: a range of walks and tours designed to suit all budgets, interests and trip lengths. These walks, driving tours and site excursions cover the destination's most classic attractions as well as a range of lesser-known sights, while food and drink stops for refreshments en route are highlighted in boxes. If you're not sure which walk to pick, our Best Walks & Tours for... feature suggests which ones work best for particular interests. The Introduction provides a destination overview, while the Directory supports the walks and tours with all the essential information you need, as well as our pick of where to stay while you are there and select restaurant listings, to complement the more low-key options given in the itineraries.

About the author

Pocket Rough Guide Ireland Walks & Tours was updated by Kate Drynan. It builds on previous work by Patrick Kinsella, a UK-based writer and former resident of Limerick and Dublin, who has a degree in Irish Studies and Kinsale-based author Alannah Hopkin. The routes in Dublin, Belfast, and counties Wicklow, Sligo and Donegal were originally written by Tara Stubbs, who has a PhD in Irish literature and culture from Oxford University.

Help us update

We've gone to a lot of effort to ensure that this edition of the **Pocket Rough Guide Ireland Walks & Tours** is accurate and up-to-date. However, things change – places get "discovered", opening hours are notoriously fickle, restaurants and rooms raise prices or lower standards. If you feel we've got it wrong or left something out, we'd like to know, and if you can remember the address, the price, the hours, the phone number, so much the better.

Please send your comments with the subject line "**Pocket Rough Guide Ireland Walks & Tours Update**" to mail@uk.roughguides.com. We'll acknowledge all contributions and send a copy of the next edition (or any other Rough Guide if you prefer) for the very best emails.

Credits

Pocket Rough Guide Ireland Walks & Tours
Editor/Updater: Kate Drynan
Authors: Alannah Hopkin, Tara Stubbs, Patrick Kinsella
Picture Manager: Tom Smyth
Cartography: Katie Bennett
Head of DTP and Pre-Press: Rebeka Davies
Head of Publishing: Sarah Clark
Photo credits: Break Out Pictures 137; British Tourist Authority 96/97; Chris Hill/Tourism Ireland 10/11, 28/29; Corbis 27; Corrie Wingate/Apa Publications 6ML, 6BC, 7T, 7MR, 7M, 7MR, 12, 13R, 12/13, 14, 15R, 14/15, 16, 17R, 16/17, 18/19, 20, 20/21, 22, 22/23, 24, 25L, 26, 30, 31, 32, 33R, 32/33, 34, 35, 39R, 38/39, 40, 40/41, 41R, 42, 42/43, 43R, 44, 45R, 44/45, 70, 70/71, 71L, 72, 72/73, 73L, 74/75, 76, 77, 78, 79, 80, 81, 82, 83, 84, 85, 86, 87L, 86/87, 88, 89L, 88/89, 90, 91L, 90/91, 111, 124, 124/125, 125L, 126, 127, 128, 129, 130, 131, 132/133, 136; Dreamstime 46, 61, 66/67, 105, 110, 116; Fáilte Ireland 49R, 48/49, 112, 118, 134; Glyn Genin/Apa Publications 6TL, 6MC, 24/25, 38, 47, 48, 50, 50/51, 52/53, 53L, 56, 58, 59, 60, 62/63, 64B, 64T, 65L, 64/65, 68, 69; Granville Hotel 98/99; iStock 19R, 36/37, 57, 92, 93, 122; James Street South 118T; Kevin Cummins/Apa Publications 21R, 54, 55, 94, 95L, 94/95, 123; Leonardo 102, 103, 104, 107, 108/109, 114/115, 117, 121; Northern Ireland Tourist Board 23L, 97L, 119, 120; Shutterstock 1, 4T, 4L, 4C, 4BR, 8/9, 27T, 106, 115T; Sligo Tourism 135; Stephen Power/Tourism Ireland 52; Tourism Ireland Imagery 18L, 96, 100/101, 113
Cover credits: Cliffs of Moher **Markus Mainka/Shutterstock**

Printed in Czech Republic

All Rights Reserved
© 2023 Apa Digital AG
License edition © Apa Publications Ltd UK

First edition 2023

This book was produced using **Typefi** automated publishing software.

No part of this book may be reproduced, stored in a retrieval system or transmitted in any form or means electronic, mechanical, photocopying, recording or otherwise, without prior written permission from Apa Publications.

Distribution

UK, Ireland and Europe
Apa Publications (UK) Ltd
sales@roughguides.com
United States and Canada
Ingram Publisher Services
ips@ingramcontent.com
Australia and New Zealand
Booktopia
retailer@booktopia.com.au
Worldwide
Apa Publications (UK) Ltd
sales@roughguides.com

Special sales, content licensing and copublishing

Rough Guides can be purchased in bulk quantities at discounted prices. We can create special editions, personalised jackets and corporate imprints tailored to your needs.
sales@roughguides.com
http://roughguides.com

Index

MAP LEGEND

★ Place of interest

● Start of tour

→ Tour & route direction

❶ Recommended sight

◔ Recommended restaurant/café

ℹ Tourist information

⚑ Statue/monument

✉ Main post office

🚌 Main bus station

Four Courts LUAS tram line

– ∙ – National boundry

∙ – – County boundry

Park

Important building

Hotel

Transport hub

Shop / market

Pedestrian area

Urban area

NOTES